The Easy-ish Way To Quit Smoking

by
Ian Rowland

———————————

Publication

The Easy-ish Way To Quit Smoking

by Ian Rowland

1st edition

Copyright © 2020 Ian Rowland. All rights reserved.
ISBN 978 1 9162408 1 0

Published by Ian Rowland Limited.

All rights reserved. This publication may not be copied or reproduced in whole or in part by any means or in any manner whatsoever without the written permission of the author.

Dedication

I dedicate this book to anyone who has an addiction and also to their loved ones, family and friends.

Let's build a world without addiction.

Yours For Free >

This booklet is available free of charge from:
www.ianrowlandtraining.com

It's about what we can all do, every day, to build a world free from addiction. Despite the subject matter, the tone is positive and hopeful, not depressing.

Please download it, copy and share!

A Quick Note About Me

I do three things so I have three websites.

www.ianrowland.com

This is about my work as a professional writer. In simple terms, I offer a complete 'start-to-finish' writing and publishing service. Technical writing, business, sales, marketing, creative... you name it, I've done it! I offer 35+ years experience across all media. In my career, I've helped more companies to sell a greater range of goods and services than anyone else you're likely to meet. I'm also a 'ghostwriter'! If you've got a book inside you, I can write it for you or guide you through the self-publishing process.

- - -

www.coldreadingsuccess.com

My website devoted to the art, science and joy of cold reading and what I call 'cold reading for business'. As well as providing free information and downloads, the site tells you about my three books on cold reading and the training I offer.

- - -

www.ianrowlandtraining.com

All about my talks and training for conferences, corporate groups and private clients. Main subjects include:

- The Practical Persuasion Method.
- Creative Problem-Solving.
- Leadership, Presence And Charisma.
- Unlock Your Mind.
- Be A Genius!
- Cold Reading For Business.

I also offer bespoke training packages to suit *your* needs. Clients to date include the FBI, Google, Coca-Cola, Unilever, the Ministry Of Defence, the British Olympics Team, the Crown Estate and many more. Full details on the site.

About My Addiction Fixer Books

A Range Of Books (With Some Overlap)

I've written a range of books about creating a world without addictions.

This book, 'The Easy-ish Way To Quit Smoking' has a self-explanatory title. I have other books on how to lose weight and get fit, and deal with alcohol problems. These books overlap to some extent because sometimes the same information is relevant to different addictions.

I've also written a short booklet called 'Let's End Addiction', which is completely free. It's about the things we can all do, every day, to create a world free from the human carnage of addiction. It's available from www.ianrowlandtraining.com in Kindle and pdf formats.

Please Tell Your Friends

If you want to tell your friends about me and this book, which I hope you will, it helps me if you send them to my own website rather than to the lovely people at Amazon:

www.ianrowlandtraining.com

I *have* made this book available on Amazon (paperback only) because these days people think that if a book's not on Amazon it doesn't exist!

However, it's nicer for me if people order from my own website, where you will also find the Kindle version, extra information, free downloads, related products and discount deals not available elsewhere.

So, please direct your friends to me rather than to Amazon if at all possible.

Thank you!

Contents

Part One: How To Quit Smoking — 11

Step 1: The Want Fix — 12
    A Different Way To Feel Good — 12
    Get To Know Your Fixer — 14
    Preparing For The Want Fix — 15
    Maintain The Relationship — 18
    Isn't Talking To Yourself Crazy? — 21
    Fake Happy Or Real? — 22

Step 2: Overcoming Dependency — 24
    The Story Of Dependency — 24
    Overcoming Dependency — 25
    The PAT Process — 26
    PAT Process (1): Plan Ahead — 26
    PAT Process (2): Three Days To Freedom — 28
    PAT Process (3): Additional Notes — 29

Step 3: Habits Of Association — 30
    A Familiar Problem — 31
    The Game Of Variations — 32
    Time Re-Allocation — 33
    The Message — 34
    Tame Your Hands — 35

Step 4: Stay Great — 37
    Reflect On Your Story — 37
    Stay Positive (As Far As Possible) — 38
    Positive Language — 39
    No-No To 'Stop-Go' — 40
    Mind And Body — 40
    You're Free, Not Deprived — 41
    Feedback Loops — 42

Part Two: Additional Information	**43**
The Ideas This Book Is Based On	**44**
Smoking Hurts Health	44
Addiction Bad, Freedom Good	45
More About The Want Fix	**46**
More About Meditation	**47**
More About Staying Great	**49**
More About Positive Attitudes	**52**
Positive Language, Not Poison Language	52
Self-Doubt No, Self-Great Yes	54
Two Bits Of Psychology	58
Handling Emotional Crunch Points	59
The 'Treated Me Badly' Trap	61
Choose Your Comparisons	62
More About Benefits	**64**
(Almost Certainly) Better Health	64
You Will Feel Better	65
More Energy And Efficiency	66
Better Leisure Time	66
Better Looks, Better Skin, Nicer Teeth	66
Higher Testosterone Levels	67
Less Smell, Less Waste	67
More Money	68
You'll Be Calmer, Less Stressed	68
The One Downside	71
Overcoming Emotional Resistance	**72**
Reassuring Your Fixer	73
Freedom And The Right To Smoke	73
Why Willpower Isn't The Answer	**75**
The Mind/Computer Analogy	**76**
My Story	**77**

Introduction

Welcome to the easy-ish way to quit smoking.

Here's my promise to you.

Part One of this book involves four steps. If you read these four steps, and follow them carefully, you will find you can quit smoking fairly easily. That will be it: done, over, end of story.

It doesn't matter how long you've been smoking, how much you smoke or how many times you've tried to quit. If you've tried before and failed, it's not your fault. It's just that nobody has given you the right information. This book is not like other books or courses you may have heard of. I will give you the *correct* information — the information that gives you the power to quit smoking for good.

Well done for *wanting* to quit. It's the right choice and you'll be very glad you did.

I need to get a few introductory things out of the way and then we can look at the four steps.

Who This Book Is For

If you smoke and don't want to, this book is for you.

If you smoke and you're happy about it, and don't care about the long-term health implications or any other aspects of smoking, then maybe this book is not for you. I'm not trying to *persuade* you to quit smoking. I'm just here for people who want to quit smoking but haven't yet found a good way to do it.

That said, if you claim to be perfectly happy that you're a smoker, think about it for a moment. You're basically saying you're happy to be the compliant, obedient mind slave of the tobacco companies, giving them money in return for something that will probably cause you to die prematurely from something horrible, painful and disgusting, such as lung cancer or obstructive pulmonary disease.

I think you deserve better than that. You might want to take a look at the section in Part Two called 'Overcoming Emotional Resistance'.

What I Mean By 'Smoking'

There are many different ways of using tobacco or getting a 'hit' of nicotine. Some people smoke cigarettes, cigars or a pipe. Some use a hookah, chew tobacco or have taken to vaping. Wikipedia's page on tobacco consumption lists about eighteen different options. It's a bizarre tribute to human ingenuity that we have devised so many ways to do something seriously unhealthy that nobody needs to do at all.

In this book, I'm going to use 'smoking' as a catch-all term to mean *any* habitual use of tobacco or nicotine. I am also going to use cigarettes as my default example, just for ease of explanation. However, let me be clear: no matter how you use tobacco or get your 'hits' of nicotine, the steps in this book will enable you to quit. Forever.

What Does Easy-ish Mean?

Achieving any significant change in your life, especially where addictions are concerned, involves *some* effort. You can't just wave a magic wand. The point is whether the amount of effort involved becomes so tiresome or annoying that you reach a breaking point, give up and go back to living the way you did before — with your addiction intact.

In this book, the four steps I'm going to describe involve a *bit* of effort, but never enough to trigger your 'to heck with it' response (or any equivalent expression) so you abandon the process and decide to carry on smoking instead. This is what I mean by 'easy-ish': not as easy as waving a magic wand but sufficiently easy for you to see it through and beat your addiction once and for all.

I once read a story about a man who wanted to lose weight. He joined a local gym, had one session with a fitness trainer and went home. Later that day, he cancelled his membership and sent the trainer a note saying, "Forget it, I've decided to stay fat." This is what happens when the solution seems harder than the addiction. I don't want this sort of thing to happen when I help people to overcome their addictions. This is why I always take the 'easy-ish' approach.

- - -

Okay, that's all the introductory stuff done. Let's look at the four steps that will enable you to quit smoking forever, the easy-ish way. Exciting, isn't it?!

You're Great

Just before we start, let's get a few things straight.

You're great.

If you smoke, this doesn't mean that you're weak, lazy or lack willpower. There's nothing wrong with you and you're just as good as anyone else. If you've tried to quit smoking before without success, relax. It's not your fault. You just weren't given the right information. You can't do *anything* if people don't give you the correct info.

You *can* quit smoking and you don't need hypnosis or an amazing amount of willpower (and willpower wouldn't work anyway). You also don't need patches, gum or any type of tobacco substitute.

I will keep these promises to you.

How This Book Works

In Part One, I'll get straight to the point and explain how to quit smoking in four steps. I've tried to keep Part One as short as I can.

In Part Two, I'll give you more information about various aspects of overcoming tobacco addiction. You might find some of these sections useful and interesting. I've kept all this extra information separate in order to keep Part One as brief as possible.

If you're interested in who I am, and how I came up with the stuff in this book, you can read 'My Story' at the end of Part Two.

Part One: How To Quit Smoking

In Part One, I'll explain how to overcome your addiction to tobacco or nicotine the easy-ish way. It involves four steps.

Important - Please Read!

I have no medical or therapeutic qualifications.

If you are going to make any significant changes in your life, you should first go to see your doctor or physician. Discuss the changes you intend to make and take their advice.

I do not accept responsibility for any aspect of your health. You should not regard anything in this book as medical advice. The contents of this book are only offered as personal testimony, opinion and information. I do not promise or guarantee any specific results or outcome. If you take any of my advice, you do so entirely at your risk and on the basis that every individual is different so results may vary.

Step 1: The Want Fix

A Different Way To Feel Good

The story with all addictions is the same: you have learned to use a particular substance or activity to change your emotional state. For example, you might eat sugary foods to comfort yourself, smoke a cigarette to cope with stress or gamble a lot because you enjoy the excitement.

Using these substances or activities certainly *works*. Unfortunately, they aren't a *good* way of achieving the desired result because they have bad consequences. Smoking, as you know, makes it far more likely you'll suffer lots of really grim and painful health problems, lung cancer just being one of many.

Here's the good news: you can learn to achieve the same results *without* the harmful substance or activity. It doesn't matter which type of 'feel good' result you're trying to achieve: cheer yourself up, cope with stress, avoid boredom, give yourself a treat, enjoy your leisure time, soothe your mind or something else. You can learn to get the same results, or even *better* results, without harming yourself or your health.

The only reason it seems difficult to do this is because nobody ever shows you the right way to do it. This is why so many people think that giving up smoking, for example, has to involve hypnosis, self-denial or huge amounts of willpower. Not true (and willpower wouldn't work anyway). All you need is a really great, powerful way to change how *one* part of your mind works. This is what I'm going to share with you.

The technique I'm going to describe was pioneered back in the 1950s by a brilliant therapist called Virginia Satir. She called it 'parts integration' and you can read more about it in Part Two if you want. I have slightly modified this therapeutic technique and I call it the Want Fix (because you're fixing how to get what you want).

This technique is *remarkably* effective. I promise that if you read this section carefully, taking in all the details, and then try the Want Fix for yourself, you will be *delighted* at how well it works.

The Want Fix And Smoking

I don't know when you started smoking or why. However, it's almost certainly true that you started smoking *to achieve a change in your emotional state*. In other words, to feel better about yourself or about some aspect of your life.

Here are a few examples you may be able to relate to. Perhaps when you were growing up you got the habit from someone in your family or a friend. They made smoking seem fairly normal or enjoyable and you wanted to 'bond' with them or not feel left out by refusing. Alternatively, perhaps at some point in your life you wanted to 'fit in' with a particular group or social circle, most of whom smoked.

Maybe smoking was just part of your teenage exploration of 'adult' fun, or you tried smoking as a way to deal with some emotional gaps or give yourself a bit of pleasure. Some smokers say they just felt bored and smoking seemed like a good idea at the time or they heard it would help them to deal with stress.

Whatever the specific details, the underlying pattern remains the same: there was a point in your life when you started using tobacco to achieve a happier emotional state. This *may* still be one part of why you smoke. Alternatively, this original reason for smoking may no longer be relevant. Perhaps today you smoke simply because you're addicted and quitting seems hard.

In Step 1, I'm going to show you how to change the way one part of your mind works. As a result, you will be able to achieve happier emotional states *without* using tobacco.

Whether you feel this step is relevant to your own situation or not, please work through it before you move on to Step 2. It's a wonderful technique to know about and you might find it useful in several areas of your life.

Okay, are you ready? Are you ready to learn about this incredible way to go into your own mind and make a *small* change that makes a *big* difference? A technique that gives you the power to overcome *any* negative habit or behaviour?

Good! Just turn the page!

Get To Know Your Fixer

You know that different parts of your body do different things. Your legs are pretty good for moving around, your hands are good at lighting up a cigarette and so on. Well, it's the same with your mind. Different parts of your mind do different things. There is one part of your mind that does a very special job: it constantly tries to keep you happy and feeling good. I'm going to refer to this part of your mind as your Fixer.

Whenever you feel disappointed, frustrated or annoyed, your Fixer tries to make you feel good again. Also, if you're just feeling a bit down, your Fixer tries to make sure you get some pleasure or a sense of reward.

How does your Fixer try to cheer you up? You already know the answer. If you like drinking alcohol, it works out the quickest way for you to get some booze. If you like smoking, it figures out the best and quickest way for you to get a 'hit' of nicotine. Whatever you're into — gambling, eating junk food or anything else — your Fixer uses it to make you feel better.

By the way, it doesn't matter whether or not you think this part of your mind, your Fixer, really exists. If you prefer, you can just regard it as a model, a metaphor or a way of representing an idea. It doesn't make any difference to the Want Fix.

Your Fixer takes care of you 24 hours a day, 7 days a week. It's really good at what it does, never stops and never *can* stop. Unfortunately, there are two big problems with the way your Fixer does its job.

The first problem is that your Fixer only understands short-term results. It doesn't understand or care about long-term consequences. All it cares about is fixing your mood *now*.

The second problem is that your Fixer uses whatever it has learned are the fastest, most reliable ways to make you feel good again. Your Fixer doesn't care whether these are smart, advisable or healthy ways to cheer you up. It just uses whatever it has learned usually *works*.

Here's the great news: you can *negotiate* with your Fixer and ask it to do its job in a different way. This is what the Want Fix is all about.

Preparing For The Want Fix

Just before we get to the actual Want Fix process, there's a little bit of preparation for you to do.

First if all, if you don't like the name 'Fixer', you can call this part of your mind anything else you like: your Mood Guru, Emotional Controller, Inner You, Mind Maestro... whatever you want. Some of my clients (that I help with smoking or other addiction issues) have come up with some pretty imaginative alternative names! All that matters is that you have *some* way of referring to it. In this book, I'll carry on referring to this part of your mind as your Fixer.

You will also need some way of *visualising* this part of your mind. It's entirely up to you how you do this. You can see your Fixer (or whatever you call it/him/her) as:

- A miniature version of you sitting somewhere in your head or your body.

- A mystical or spiritual entity of some kind, like a 'ghost' version of you that drives your choices.

- An abstract presence, like a source of light or energy.

- A robot, full of wires and circuits deep inside your brain, programmed to keep you happy.

- A well-meaning friend.

- Someone at a large control desk, full of screens and dials, trying to operate your mental machinery.

- A favourite celebrity or star who lives in one part of your mind and takes care of all your 'fixing' for you.

Choose whatever visualisation works for you. All that matters is that you have a way of visualising your Fixer that you like.

Good. You have a way of referring to your Fixer and visualising it. Now you're ready for the Want Fix.

The Five Parts

The Want Fix involves asking your Fixer to do its job in a different way.

I'm going to explain the Want Fix in five parts. It's best to read through the whole process, so you know how it goes, before you actually try it.

Want Fix (1): Meditate

You need to find about 15 minutes of peace and quiet. Choose any time and place where you can relax and meditate. Just sitting in a comfy armchair or on the edge of your bed is fine.

Relax and focus on your breathing for a while. Enjoy slow, deep breaths, in and out. If you know how to meditate, great. If not, ask a friend, read about meditation online or see section in Part 2: 'More About Meditation'.

After you have focused on your breathing for a while, say you want to communicate with your Fixer (or whatever name you prefer). This all takes place inside your mind and only involves your inner voice. You *can* speak out loud if you want to but your inner voice is enough.

Your Fixer doesn't have a voice so it can't talk. Invite your Fixer to give you *some* sort of signal that it is listening to you. The response will just be a feeling of some kind: a twitch of your hand or fingers, a sense of part of your mind or body 'lighting up' with attention, a feeling of energy or something else. Just wait until you feel *something* to indicate your Fixer is listening and responding.

Once you have made contact with your Fixer, you can carry on.

Want Fix (2): Give Credit And Gratitude

Give your Fixer *credit* for all the great work it does and express your *gratitude*. In your own words, say something like this:

> "I want to thank you for all the great work you do! I know you work really hard for me, constantly trying to make me happy when I don't feel good. You do a great job and you never let me down. I really appreciate the work you do. Thank you for looking after me so well!"

Wait for your Fixer to give you some sort of feeling or sensation by way of response. Once you have given credit and expressed your gratitude, you can continue.

Want Fix (3): Negotiate

Next, make it clear you are *not* going to ask your Fixer to stop doing its job. This wouldn't be a successful approach because it *can't* stop. Ask your Fixer to carry on doing what it does but in a slightly different way. Using your own words, negotiate with it like this:

> "I am not going to ask you to stop doing what you do. I love what you do for me and want you to carry on!
>
> However, I'd like you to do your job in a slightly different way. Some of the methods you use at the moment provide fake, short-term happiness, but they have long-term results that actually make me *un*happy. For example, I don't really want to be a smoker. It's expensive, seriously unhealthy and just not a good idea. I sometimes feel unhappy about it.
>
> I don't want fake, short-term happiness with bad consequences. I want long-term happiness with good consequences. So, please can I ask you to use some other ways of making me feel good?"

Wait for your Fixer to respond in some way. As before, this won't be in words. It will just be a feeling or a sensation of some kind.

Want Fix (4): Suggest Better Ways To Feel Good

Suggest ways in which your Fixer can help you to feel good that will *not* have bad long-term consequences. Obviously, only you know what will work for you. Here are a few possibilities to get you started:

> Go for a good walk / visit the beach / go for a drive / visit a place of outstanding natural beauty.
>
> Call a friend you haven't spoken to for a while / meet up with friends and have fun (without smoking) / chat to a friend online.
>
> Work on your car or bike, tackle some DIY, work on a practical project where you make, build or repair something.
>
> Play a musical instrument or learn how to / write a short story / devote some time to a craft or hobby.
>
> Play with your pet / do some 'de-clutter' housework you find satisfying / do some gardening or tend to your houseplants.
>
> Bake or cook something (preferably non-fattening).

Watch something funny online / get stuck into a good book / watch TV or listen to a radio show, audio book or podcast.

Feel pampered in some way, such as getting your hair or nails done. Meditate, do some yoga, sip green tea, become enlightened and solve the mysteries of the universe.

Do something silly, fun and frivolous. Alternatively, study for a qualification of some kind and gain a marketable skill.

Join a local special interest group (books, drama, board games, vintage car restoration, ... whatever you're into). Take part in a faith-based activity at your place of worship if you have one.

Make love with your partner / watch a classic movie / have a nap / take a shower. (I'm listing these as separate choices but, hey, if you can combine all four, great!)

Do some charity or voluntary work so your focus is other people instead of yourself.

Simply lie down for a bit or enjoy a short nap.

Just talk to your Fixer and suggest a few ways to make you feel good and lift your mood that do *not* have bad long-term consequences. You are helping your Fixer to do its job in a new, different and better way.

As before, wait for a response from your Fixer.

Want Fix (5): Give More Thanks And End The Session

Thank your Fixer for listening to you and for responding to your suggestions.

Repeat your acknowledgement of all the good work your Fixer does for you. Repeat your thanks and make it clear that you want your Fixer to carry on doing its important and excellent work but in a slightly different way.

Having completed these steps, finish off with some more meditation and breathing exercises. In your own time, allow yourself to come out of the meditative state and back into your normal, conscious awareness of your surroundings.

You have completed your first Want Fix session! Well done! I hope you found it satisfying and enjoyable.

Maintain The Relationship

Just talking to your Fixer once won't work. It's important for you to maintain an *ongoing relationship*. In fact, you should have four types of sessions with your Fixer. Let's look at each of the four.

Regular Reminders

On a regular basis, repeat the Want Fix I've just outlined. Meditate, get in touch with your Fixer and go over the same basic points: praise and thanks, negotiation, suggestions and a bit more thanks to finish off.

Having these 'reminder' sessions once a day is ideal, especially when you first quit smoking. If this isn't practical for you, aim for at least two or three sessions a week. They don't have to take long. I generally choose to meditate for about fifteen minutes if I have the time but if not I'll just have a much shorter session lasting five minutes or less. You might find that short sessions are all you need.

Each session is a chance to reinforce the new direction you want to take. It's also another opportunity to praise and encourage your Fixer — and we all work better with regular encouragement!

Handling Challenges: The Mental Movie

As well as regular reminder sessions with your Fixer, have an extra session whenever a challenging situation is coming up. A 'challenging situation' is one in which you might feel tempted to go back to your old ways and smoke.

For example, let's say you're planning to meet a friend at a place where, in the past, you tended to smoke. You can make sure this doesn't happen. All you have to do is use a powerful technique called 'The Mental Movie'.

Here's how to do it. Meditate and get in touch with your Fixer. *Anticipate* what's going to happen and ask your Fixer to handle it in a new, better way. Use your own words to say something like this:

> "Today I'm going to meet [friend] at [place] where, in the past, I usually smoked some cigarettes to feel relaxed or more sociable. Can we please do things a bit differently this time? I want to meet my friend and have a great time, share a laugh or two and come home after... but *without* smoking. Can we do it this way, please?"

Next, play a *mental movie* of the whole situation, from start to finish, the way you want it to play out. See the whole thing in your imagination. You go along, you meet your friend, you have a great time, you make your way home. It's all good — you just don't smoke anything. You are showing your Fixer a short movie of how you want things to go.

It's your mental movie so you can have fun with it. Speed it up or slow it down. Zoom in and out. Run parts of it backwards. Put some music to it: either stirring and inspirational or silly and light-hearted. Exaggerate some elements. Try different cinematic styles: a black and white movie from the silent era / sepia tinted / 50s Technicolor / expressionist / film noir / cartoon / Western / romantic comedy / action adventure / atmospheric thriller. It's all happening in your mind so you can imagine it any way you want!

Then go along and enjoy your meeting with your friend. You'll find you enjoy it just as much as you would normally — but with very little or no inclination to smoke!

The Mental Movie technique works almost like magic. It's easy to use yet very powerful and effective. Supposedly 'challenging' situations will be challenging no more!

Praise Sessions

Whenever your Fixer does well, and keeps you feeling good *without* using the old methods that involve smoking, take the time to thank your Fixer. This only needs to take a minute or two, although you can spend longer if you want. Communicate with your Fixer in the usual way and then, in your own words, say something like this:

> "I just want to thank you for the way you handled that situation today, and the way that we did [non-smoking activity] instead of [smoking]. That was really good! It's exactly what I want you to do! Well done! I'm so grateful to you."

It's important to do this. When you do a good job for someone, you like it if they express a bit of gratitude, don't you?

Well, your Fixer feels the same way. When it does its job the new way, the *right* way that you have asked it to, it enjoys a bit of thanks.

Correction Sessions

Suppose there's an occasion when your Fixer looks after you in the old way. You smoke a cigarette and you feel a bit of regret afterwards. What should you do?

Have a session with your Fixer. Don't be critical. Be kind, forgiving and encouraging. In your own words, say something like this:

> "I smoked today. This isn't really what I want because I don't want to be addicted to nicotine any more. I really want to be a non-smoker. It's all right — you're learning new ways to keep me happy and this is a process of adjustment. It's obviously going to take some time. When I'm in that situation again, please can you handle it this way [suggest a better way of dealing with it]. I'd really appreciate it. You do great work, and I know you're going to get even better at it as time goes by!"

Always talk to your Fixer in your own words and using your own way of expressing yourself. I'm just offering general guidelines. Always keep the tone positive, grateful and encouraging.

Isn't Talking To Yourself Crazy?

Some people say things like this about the Want Fix:

> "Isn't it crazy to talk to myself?"

> "I would feel stupid just sitting there talking to me."

First of all, there's nothing wrong with self-talk. Millions of people do it every day. There is nothing wrong with it in psychological or psychiatric terms.

Secondly, you're not just 'talking to yourself'. You are using a valid therapeutic technique to connect with a part of your own mind. You're doing it to achieve a positive change in your behaviour and your life. There's nothing wrong with this. In any case, nobody else has to know about it! Negotiating with your Fixer is something you can do on your own when there's nobody else around.

Some people hire me to mentor them through the process of quitting smoking. I've never yet had a client who couldn't find some quiet, private time to meditate and communicate with their Fixer. It's not crazy and nobody else needs to know what you're doing.

Fake Happy Or Real?

The Want Fix always works. Literally everyone can benefit from it.

Take a moment to think about this. You have an innate desire to feel happy, content and fulfilled — in fact, to feel as good as you can, as often as you can. This is just part of how we're all wired up.

Your Fixer / Controller / Inner You (whatever you're calling it) knows it can make you feel better using nicotine. However, this method only creates *fake* happiness for a *short* time. In the long-term, it has bad consequences. For one thing, you're aware that this not-very-good method will almost certainly lead to serious health problems that you will *not* feel happy about at all.

By using the Want Fix, you are suggesting ways your Fixer can help you feel good *all* the time *without* harmful consequences. (When I say 'all the time', this is a slight exaggeration. Life always has its ups and downs. I'm really saying 'as much of the time as possible'.)

It's a simple choice. When it comes to feeling good, do you want *fake happiness* for a *short* time? Or *genuine* happiness almost *all* the time?

It's Going To Happen Anyway

There's one thing about your Fixer that it's important to understand. You don't get a choice about whether it affects your life or not. It is going to drive your behaviour whether you want it to or not. It never stops and can't stop.

You can believe it's real or not. You can believe it governs a lot of your behaviour or not. Regardless of what you choose to believe, it's going to be there, working 24/7 and doing its best to keep you feeling good.

The only choice you get is this: does your Fixer use the old ways to keep you happy (that lead to bad results like lung cancer and emphysema) or new, better ways that take you to a happier, better place *without* any bad consequences? This is your choice. The car is moving along regardless of what you think. All you get to choose is the destination: fake, short-term happiness that doesn't last and leads to problems, or real, long-term happiness that lasts almost all the time.

Progress Check

This was Step 1: 'The Want Fix'. It was about negotiating with your Fixer so that it will use different methods to make you feel good. Basically, it's about realising you don't want *fake* happiness for a *short* time. You want *genuine* happiness *all* the time.

If you want more background information, see Part 2 of this book: 'More About The Want Fix'.

What's next? Well, the next aspect of addiction you need to understand is *dependency* and how to overcome it. This is what Step 2 is all about.

Step 2: Overcoming Dependency

Step 1 was about one aspect of addiction: using a substance to achieve a happier emotional state. Now that you know about the Want Fix, you know how to deal with this aspect of addiction. So far, so good.

In Step 2, we're going to look at another aspect of addictive behaviour: dependency. Let's look at how it arises and how to overcome it.

The Story Of Dependency

Here's a *very* simplified account of dependency.

There are receptors in your body that monitor your blood. They act like soldiers on sentry duty. When everything's all right, they send signals to your brain saying, 'Everything's normal. You're fine.' Whenever there seems to be something wrong with your blood, such as your blood being contaminated in some way, they send different signals: 'Red alert! Something's gone wrong! You need to fix this!'

Some substances can play a nasty trick on you. They are able to 're-wire' these receptors so they don't work properly. Nicotine is one very good example. The correct amount of nicotine to have in your bloodstream at any given time is 'zero'. This is the default setting you were born with. It's also why most people, when they try their first cigarette, feel a bit nauseous.

Nicotine can chemically alter your receptors so they don't work correctly any more. They start to regard a given quantity of nicotine as the normal amount to have in your blood. When the amount falls below this 'normal' level, they send a panic signal. 'Alert! Nicotine levels dropping! Fix this!' The result is that you crave a cigarette.

This is what we mean by dependency. You *depend* on the substance just to feel normal. This dependency leads to a pattern of behaviour. You get the 'alert' signal and respond by getting more nicotine (or whichever substance you happen to be addicted to). As nicotine continues to damage your receptors, the problem gets worse and your dependency increases.

To overcome an addiction to nicotine, or anything else that damages your receptors in a similar way, you have to go through the process of *withdrawal*. This means breaking the behavioural cycle of *alert* triggering *response*. When you manage to do this, your receptors will gradually repair themselves and start to work normally again.

Overcoming Dependency

We can divide all addictions into two groups.

Group 1: Addictions that do not involve a substance (such as gambling, work, internet, video games).

Group 2: Addictions that *do* involve a substance (such as sugar, alcohol, nicotine or drugs).

Group 2 addictions can be subdivided into three groups, based on what's needed to overcome them:

(a) **The Want Fix is enough**. Your dependency is so mild that the Want Fix is all you need.

(b) **Want Fix + Withdrawal**. You need the Want Fix and, in addition, a way to handle withdrawal. You can manage the withdrawal on your own without medical supervision.

(c) **Want Fix + Withdrawal Under Medical Supervision**. The dependency is so strong that the withdrawal process causes strong, toxic reactions in the body and requires medical supervision.

Most people who want to quit smoking are in either group 2 (a) or 2 (b). If you feel you need a little extra help overcoming your dependency on nicotine, this section is for you. I'm going to describe something called the PAT Process that will help you to overcome your dependency.

If you are in group 2 (c), the PAT Process won't be enough. You will need qualified medical supervision to manage the withdrawal process.

GROUP 1: No substance abuse

GROUP 2: Substance abuse
Levels of dependency:
- 2 (a) Want Fix is enough
- 2 (b) Want Fix + withdrawal process (by yourself)
- 2 (c) Want Fix + withdrawal process
 (requiring medical supervision)

The PAT Process

This section is for you if:

- You have a dependency on nicotine.
- You think you can probably manage the withdrawal yourself.

In other words, you are in group 2 (b) as defined on the previous page.

This section does not apply to you if you are in group 2 (c). You will need trained, medical supervision to manage the withdrawal process.

Assuming you are in group 2 (b), what's the best way to overcome your dependency? Here's the best, most consistently successful approach I know. It's called the PAT process, which stands for Planned Aware Transition.

PAT Process (1): Plan Ahead

Here's the good news: no matter how strong your dependency is, you can break it in *three days*. If you can just manage to go without nicotine for three days, you will have beaten the dependency and it will have lost its power over you. You will have broken the 'alert / response' cycle I described. In addition, your damaged receptors will start to heal and repair themselves so they start working properly again. They will once more realise that the right amount of nicotine to have in your bloodstream is 'none'.

It doesn't matter how long you've been smoking, how many cigarettes you smoke in a day or anything else. When you go three days without nicotine, you will break its hold on you. Your addiction response will 'burn out', so to speak, and you will be free from your addiction.

I'm not saying these three days will be the happiest days of your life. However, you can get through them if you go about it the right way.

First of all, you need to find a block of three days that you can devote, completely and exclusively, to overcoming your dependency. It's up to you how you schedule these three days and a lot will depend on your personal circumstances. For example, if you have a Monday-to-Friday job, maybe your three days could be a weekend plus either a Friday or a Monday off work.

Next, plan *where* you are going to spend these three days, which is very much a matter of personal preference.

Some people go for the 'Home Sanctuary' option, which basically means spending three days at home. It's a safe and familiar environment, you have all your usual ways of passing the time around you and you can sleep in your own bed. This obviously won't suit you if you feel, for whatever reason, that your home environment isn't very conducive to overcoming dependency. For example, you may feel it's full of cues and associations that make it harder not to smoke.

Others prefer the 'Change Of Scenery' option. This involves going away somewhere nice that will provide a complete change of scenery and mood. This could involve renting a holiday cottage, staying somewhere near the beach, visiting a friend or relative, going on a retreat or just checking into a hotel somewhere interesting or very remote. Some people feel the change of environment helps them in emotional terms to break with past habits. New place, new feelings, new you.

If you choose the 'Change Of Scenery' option, you need to exercise a little care. Many places look idyllic in the adverts or brochures but turn out to be rather disappointing in real life. Any negative feelings of dismay will make it harder for you to overcome your dependency. For this reason, do your best to make *absolutely sure* the location you choose will be suitable for the purpose. Choosing a place that you know will be suitable based on past experience is a good idea. However, you need to avoid places that have addictive triggers and associations for you.

Next, you need to get creative! Arm yourself with as many ways to pass the time as you possibly can. The point is to make sure that for three days you never, ever feel bored — not even for a second — and you *always* have something to do. Just line up all the best ways you can think of to fill the time and keep yourself occupied.

How you choose to spend your time during these three days is clearly a matter of personal preference. Here are just a few options: TV, movies, video games, reading, hobbies, crafts, long walks, exercise, sleeping, study, fun, social time, meditation, housework, gardening, baking, jigsaw puzzles, fishing, writing, painting... and so on. Prepare as many ways to fill the time as you can think of. The only rule is that you cannot use *any* addictive substance.

Bear in mind that during the three days of the PAT Process you will sometimes feel that time is passing *remarkably* slowly! It's not unusual for every minute to seem like an hour. You may well find yourself staring at the clock in disbelief that time can pass so unhelpfully slowly!

During these three days, do not have any supply of nicotine available. Get rid of it all. You won't be needing it. The same goes for any other addictive substance.

PAT Process (2): Three Days To Freedom

You've planned your three days and made sure you have lots of ways of passing the time.

Day 1 arrives. The rules are simple: for these three days, you can spend your time doing anything you want so long as you don't use *any* addictive substance. None at all.

The crucial part is to *anticipate* exactly what's going to happen and how you will respond.

Here's what will happen: the receptors in your body — the ones that have been damaged by nicotine — will start sending panic messages to your brain. 'Emergency! Levels of nicotine are getting dangerously low! You need to do something *now* to fix the problem!' These messages may be accompanied by physical signs of stress or anxiety.

When this happens, relax, stay in the moment and remain entirely aware of what's happening and why. Remain calm and focused. Talk to yourself the way you would talk to a friend who is very concerned for you but is mistaken. You can do this out loud or you can meditate and use your internal voice. In a calm, gentle way, say: "I know what's happening. There are damaged receptors in my body that are sending incorrect signals. In reality, there's nothing wrong and I don't need to do anything. The receptors that are sending these alarm signals are wrong. They are not working properly. The correct amount of nicotine for me to take on board right now is zero."

From time to time, your damaged receptors will try again. This is understandable. From their point of view, so to speak, they are doing their job: alerting you to a serious problem just as they would if, say, you weren't getting enough oxygen. Each time they try to send this faulty 'alert' signal to your brain, stay calm, remain aware of what's happening, talk to yourself and repeat the same message — you are aware of what's happening, you understand why you are experiencing these signals, there's nothing actually wrong, *faulty* receptors are sending *incorrect* messages as if there's an emergency when, in fact, there's no emergency at all and everything's fine.

Enjoy your complete control over this situation. The damaged receptors can shout all they like and have a tantrum but they cannot physically move your hands. They cannot make you reach for a cigarette or do anything else. You have *total* control. They have *none*. Each time they come back with another false alarm, just calmly face them down, re-state the facts and watch their weak, pathetic, defeated powerlessness. There is nothing they can do.

As you progress through Day 1 and maybe part of Day 2, the false alarms from your damaged receptors will increase in frequency and intensity until they reach a peak. From that point on, they will gradually recede, fade and get weaker. You will experience fewer of these faulty alerts and they will become less intense. Look forward to witnessing this process.

This will not be a pleasant experience but you can get through it. The key is to anticipate exactly what's going to happen and how you're going to respond. The rest of the time, just keep yourself occupied and pass the time however you prefer.

After three days, your receptors will have stopped or very nearly stopped sending these faulty alert messages. Any alerts you do still feel will be far fainter and less intense than they used to be. The receptors in your body will slowly start to repair themselves so they give accurate signals once again. They will once more regard 'zero' as the correct amount of nicotine to have in your bloodstream.

Congratulations! You have overcome your dependency! You don't need patches or substitutes, hypnosis, willpower or anything else. Just the Planned, Aware Transition to your new life.

What you devote to this: three days.

What you get: living *the rest of your life* with freedom, choice and control instead of addiction.

PAT Process (3): Additional Notes

If the PAT process leads to great physical stress or makes you feel significantly unwell, then it's not right for you. You are in Group 2 (c) (as defined earlier) and trying to manage your own withdrawal isn't going to work. You will need qualified medical supervision. Check the resources available in your area and get the help you need. It is rare for anyone addicted to nicotine to be in Group 2 (c) but it is possible.

You may want to go through the PAT process on your own or mostly on your own. If you live alone, this is easy. If not, you'll need to figure out the best way to achieve three days of solitude or near-solitude.

Alternatively, you may want to go through the PAT process with a partner, your family, a friend or group of friends. Maybe you want their support and encouragement! This can work but you need to follow a few guidelines. People who are going to spend time with you need to be fully supportive and promise *they will not try to interfere*. In particular, they must not start offering their own suggestions about how to overcome addiction or quit smoking. This is not the time for them to start sharing stories about how a friend of theirs stopped smoking and offering advice. They need to be well informed about what you are doing and why, and to understand that you will occasionally need to concentrate, focus, meditate or talk to yourself (when you respond calmly to the false alarms).

During the three days of the PAT process, avoid social spaces such as cafes, bars, clubs and restaurants. One reason for this is that you need to stay in an environment that allows you to *control* how you pass your time. Another reason is that, for most people with an addiction, social spaces tend to have connotations of 'fun' and 'having a good time'. These aren't helpful when you're trying to overcome a dependency.

Don't go through the PAT process with someone else who is also trying to overcome the same dependency or any other. This is highly unlikely to work. If you're going to have other people around you, they should ideally be people who are not addicted to anything.

As they say on the warnings of some medication, don't plan on doing much driving or operating heavy machinery during the PAT process. During the three days, you are going to be in a rather distracted state of mind with impaired concentration. You will probably feel anxious at some times and drowsy at others. Basically, you won't be in any fit state to drive in a safe, responsible way and your judgment will be impaired. So, find other things to do.

That's it! That's the PAT Process from start to finish. This is all you need in order to break your dependency on nicotine.

Progress Check

This was Step 2: 'Overcoming Dependency'. It was about how dependency works and how to deal with it using the PAT Process: prepared, aware transition.

What's next? If you know how to use The Want Fix and The PAT Process, you have all the tools you need to overcome your addiction to tobacco or nicotine. However, there's a third aspect of smoking that we need to address: habits of association. This is what Step 3 is all about.

Step 3: Habits Of Association

A Familiar Problem

Habits of association sound like this: "I always have a cigarette when I sit down to watch my favourite show"; "I always light up when I get into work"; "I always have a smoke on Friday night after I've put the kids to bed"; "I always have a few smokes when I meet up with my friends — it wouldn't be the same if I didn't."

In other words, you have learned to associate a recurring event with nicotine. If you look it rationally, you know perfectly well that you don't *need* to smoke on any of these occasions. Millions of people enjoy the same events, or go through similar routines, without reaching for nicotine or any other addictive substance. However, addictive behaviour is anything but rational so this doesn't really help. In fact, you've probably experienced that kind of mental and emotional conflict where one part of you says 'I want to smoke' while another part of you says '...but I know I shouldn't'.

This kind of internal conflict isn't very pleasant and it's not good for you. It can all too easily lead to you disliking yourself. I'd much rather you loved yourself, felt great about yourself and took great delight in what a unique, wonderful, lovable and admirable person you are.

What you need is a good way to deal with habits of association. Fortunately, there *is* a way to do this. In fact, I've already described it. If you go back a few pages to Step 1, there was a section entitled 'Handling Challenges: The Mental Movie'. You can use the same Mental Movie technique to neutralise any habit of association.

For example, suppose you always light up a cigarette whenever you settle down to watch your favourite TV show. If you follow the steps described in The Mental Movie, you can break this habit of association very easily — or at least in a way that is easy-ish.

First, you anticipate the situation (settling down to watch your show) and mentally prepare for it. You meditate, contact your Fixer and ask it to handle the situation in a new and better way that does *not* involve smoking.

Then, in your imagination, you play the mental movie of how you would like the situation to unfold. You imagine yourself settling down in your favourite armchair, flicking the TV on and looking forward to the start of your show. You watch the show and enjoy it as normal — just without smoking. The show ends and then you go and do something else.

As I said when I described the Mental Movie technique a few pages back, don't forget to have fun with this. Since the movie only exists in your imagination, you can play around with it, see it in different cinematic styles, exaggerate some parts of the scene and so on.

The Mental Movie is a really effective and enjoyable way to deal with Habits Of Association. However, it only works if you have also worked through Step 1 'The Want Fix' and Step 2 'Overcoming Dependency'.

Note that I do not say 'this is a really good way to re-program your mind' or 'to re-program your behaviour'. Your mind does *not* work like a computer and this sort of 're-programming' analogy is seriously unhelpful. I'll address this point in more detail in Part Two of this book.

The Mental Movie technique is a great way to overcome habits of association and I hope you find it useful. However, just in case you need a little extra help, I'm going to mention some additional tools and techniques you can use.

The Game Of Variations

Another technique for breaking habits of association is to disrupt the old routine, which included smoking, and build a new one that smoking is *not* part of.

Here's a simple example. Suppose you have an office job and you always tended to light up a cigarette (either outside or in the designated area) as soon as you got to work and grabbed your first cup of coffee. You could try keeping everything the same *except* for the smoking. However, you might find this hard because there will be so many cues and sense memories that you associate with having a cigarette.

To make life a little easier, see if you can change *several* aspects of your arriving-at-work routine so that you are not *just* changing the 'smoking' part on its own. Can you arrive via a different route, do things in a different order or add a minor task you didn't include before? Instead of that first coffee, drink orange juice or something else. Instead of habitually chatting to the co-worker who smokes, chat to the one who doesn't. Instead of taking the stairs, use the lift/elevator or vice-versa. Think of anything you can add, delete or change to make a difference.

By making quite a few changes, you will feel as if you're constructing a whole new routine rather than just making a small modification to the old one. The aim is to reduce the number of links to the old routine (which included 'light up a cigarette') and build a new routine (without the cigarette).

You can do this with any routine that smoking used to be part of: your 'first thing in the morning' routine, 'going for lunch' routine, 'meeting friends' routine, 'feeling pretty fed up to be honest' routine, 'long journey in the car' routine, 'relaxing before going to bed routine' and so on. The more changes you make, the less influence the old routine (that included smoking) will have over you.

I do understand that this isn't *always* possible. There may be some routines in your life that you can't alter very much, perhaps because there are other people involved or you don't have much room for manoeuvre. However, where you *can* make quite a few changes, and build a new routine, try it and see if this helps you to break the habit of association.

Time Re-Allocation

Here's another idea that can help to break habits of association.

Consider any routine in your life that used to involve smoking. Where possible, think about the time you used to spend smoking and re-allocate it towards a different goal. Ideally, it should be the sort of goal that involves numerous small steps that, over time, build towards something worth achieving.

For example, Jack used to always take ten minutes to have a cigarette while waiting to pick his kids up from school. He re-allocated those ten minutes to learning Italian from an online language course that he could listen to on his phone. You can't learn much Italian in ten minutes but you can learn a lot over the course of a year! Or, as he would say, "In dieci minuti non puoi imparare un granché d'italiano, ma nel corso di un anno certamente si."

Jane used to always take a few minutes to smoke before going to catch her morning train to work. Although she'd never been a great reader, she'd heard that 'Orlando' by Virginia Woolf was considered a great novel and was really funny in parts. She started carrying a copy round with her and, each morning, she re-allocated her smoking time to reading another bit of 'Orlando'. She only made a small amount of progress each time. Nonetheless, she eventually finished the whole book and then went on to explore more books by the same author.

Chloe liked to smoke when she got back from her day at college. She had always enjoyed the notion of restoring, repairing and 're-purposing' things. She had bought a set of old-fashioned weighing scales from a junk sale. They were filthy, covered in rust and grime, and looked beyond salvage. Instead of smoking, she enjoyed short, ten-minute sessions that she devoted to cleaning, restoring and re-painting these antique scales. Of course, she didn't make much progress during each individual session. Her progress was actually very slow. However, after a few months had passed, the scales looked absolutely beautiful. Cleaned and restored to 'good as new' condition, they took pride of place in Chloe's kitchen.

Smoking is one way to spend your time. You have the freedom, choice and control to change how you spend that time and to channel it in a different direction. We all get given a certain amount of time in this life. It's easy to find better ways to spend your time than sucking fumes into your lungs that make it more likely you'll die prematurely from something horrible, disgusting and painful.

The Message

Here's another way to break a habit of association. It's rather sentimental but I don't think this is necessarily a bad thing. In many ways, we could all do with a bit more kindness and sentimentality in our lives rather than less.

All you need is one person in your life who doesn't smoke and who loves you or at least cares about you. It could be your spouse / partner or just a close friend. Ask them to give you a message that goes something like this, but expressed in their own words:

> "I know you're thinking about smoking right now. You're somewhere that reminds you of when you used to smoke and I understand you might feel tempted. But please don't. I care about you and I want you to give yourself the best possible chance of staying healthy. You matter to me. I want you around. Please, don't harm yourself. Cigarettes will never care about you or love you, but I do. So please don't smoke."

If they give this to you as a written note, carry it around with you so you can read it whenever you want to. Alternatively, have them record it as an audio or video message that you can store on your phone and refer to at any time.

Whenever you're trying to overcome a habit of association, take a moment to read, watch or listen to this message and remind yourself that some things in life matter more than smoking ever could.

If you honestly can't find anyone to write or record a message like this for you, here's a free offer: just ask me to do it! I'll be more than happy to write or record a message for you.

Tame Your Hands

Here's another aspect of habits of association: what do you with your hands?!

Many people who stop smoking say their hands feels strangely empty so they start to fidget and feel restless. For example, let's say you were in the habit of smoking a cigarette while watching TV. When you stop smoking, you may feel a bit distracted from the TV because your hands won't stop fidgeting. There are at least three good ways to deal with this. See which one works best for you.

Distraction

The first option is *distraction*. This means giving your hands something else to do.

For example, you could stroke your cat, shuffle cards, play with a pencil, do some knitting or hug a cushion. You could play with a rubber ball, fidget cube or any type of 'stress' toy. (As an amateur magician, I could happily keep my hands busy with a deck of cards, practising sleight of hand, for hours on end if I wanted to.)

You could also keep your hands busy by eating or snacking. However, there's no point in overcoming one problem, such as smoking, and developing another in its place, such as over-eating and making yourself unhealthily overweight.

Exercise (Plus Deliberate Tedium)

The second option is to use *hand exercises*.

Here's one example. Position your hands in a 'prayer' position so you can press the pads of your thumbs together, keeping your fingers straight. Interlace your fingers with the right forefinger on top of your left forefinger. This is position (1). Flex your fingers once. Then, keeping your thumbs as they are, re-arrange your fingers so the left forefinger is now on top of your right forefinger. This is position (2). Again, flex your fingers once. Go back to position (1) and flex your fingers twice. Switch to position (2) and flex twice. Keep on alternating, increasing the number of flexes until you're up to six.

By this point, you should be finding the whole process a bit boring, which is the whole point. If not, repeat the whole cycle, from one flex up to six. Once you are bored with it, you should find your hands are content to just do nothing for a while. If they start to get fidgety again, put them through another cycle of flexing exercises. Eventually, they'll calm down.

If you don't like this exercise, you can find others. Just search online for 'finger flexibility exercises', 'yoga for hands' and similar terms. Alternatively, make up your own little hand routines. The general point is to teach your hands that if they get fidgety, you're just going to make them do some boring exercises. They'll soon learn to keep still.

The Stare Down

The third option is to use the same technique I mentioned during the Pat Process: remain aware of what's happening, stare down your hands and enjoy their powerlessness.

If your hands get fidgety and restless, take a moment to look at them. Be completely aware of what's happening and mentally address the issue: "I know exactly what's going on. My hands are feeling restless because I used to smoke a cigarette in this situation and so my hands still have that muscle memory, but now they don't have anything to do. However, in time, they will learn to just be still and relaxed."

Look at your hands. You have *all* the power and control. Your hands can't get a cigarette or do anything else without your permission (which you are not going to give). You are in charge.

Stay focused on your hands and on this situation. The restless, fidgety feeling will intensify until it reaches a peak. After that, it will gradually fade away. If the feeling comes back, go through the same process: remain aware of what's happening and why, look at your powerless hands, stay in charge and wait for the feelings to peak and then fade.

You will only have to go through this cycle a few times before you find that restless hands just aren't a problem any more.

Progress Check

This was Step 3: 'Habits Of Association'. In this step, I offered you a few ways to deal with situations that trigger sense memories and have emotional links to smoking. You can try all of them or just one. All that matters is that you find one that works.

Step 4: Stay Great

You now have all the information you need to quit smoking forever.

In Step 1, 'The Want Fix', you learned how to change one part of your mind so you can achieve a happier emotional state *without* using tobacco.

In Step 2, 'Overcoming Dependency', you saw how to break your dependency on nicotine using the PAT Process (Planned, Aware Transition).

Finally, in Step 3, 'Habits of Association', we looked at a few good ways to deal with situations that might trigger an inclination to smoke.

Using these three steps, you can give up smoking forever. The choice you face is not complicated.

Option 1: choose to remain addicted, being a slave of the tobacco companies who take your money and (probably) your health.

Option 2: choose the opposite of addiction, which is freedom, choice and control. Keep your money and give yourself the best possible chance of staying healthy.

Twenty years ago, I chose option 2. I've never touched a cigarette since or wanted to. I hope you will make the same choice for yourself. You're worth it and you deserve to be more than Big Tobacco's mind slave, regularly poisoning yourself with a carcinogenic drug.

However, this isn't the end of the story. It's one thing to become a non-smoker. It's quite another to *stay* a non-smoker. In this final step, I want to offer you some suggestions about how to do this.

Reflect On Your Story

Once you've given up smoking, take some time to think back over the story of your addiction in emotional terms. Devote a significant amount of time to this because it's highly therapeutic and productive.

Think about why you started smoking, why it seemed like a good or appealing idea at the time. Think about the feelings that were involved. Were you trying to move away from negative feelings (such as resentment, anger, frustration, disappointment or boredom)? Or were you trying to move towards positive feelings (such as acceptance, belonging, peer group respect, pleasure and relaxation)?

Go for long walks and think all this over. Alternatively, talk about it with a friend who's good at listening (or your pet, or a qualified counsellor). Try to understand your story in emotional terms, to understand yourself and see how your addiction started and why it continued.

As you reflect on all of this, you should also learn to be more accepting of yourself. Anyone can become addicted to something. It's not a sign of weakness or a terrible character flaw. It doesn't mean you're a damaged person. It just means there was a time when you made a poor decision, had bad influences or ran out of coping mechanisms. It happens.

Having a good think about the story of your addiction is really useful, for all sorts of reasons. The more you understand about how you became addicted, the easier it becomes to avoid ever getting caught in the same trap again. It also helps you to see things in perspective and to appreciate that life is a series of chapters. You have no power to change your past but you have *all* the power to shape your future. You are the architect of all your tomorrows.

This process also helps you to accept, love and respect yourself. You're not broken and there's nothing wrong with you. You're great and just as good as anyone else. You once got addicted to something. Now you've moved on and you can enjoy the rest of your life with freedom, choice and control.

Stay Positive (As Far As Possible)

Maintaining a positive outlook on life is a profoundly important part of making sure you stay great and never taking up smoking again. Let me explain why.

If you have negotiated successfully with your Fixer, it will try to keep you feeling good using the new, positive methods you have suggested that do *not* involve nicotine. Most of the time, this should work pretty well. However, if you spur your Fixer into action very often, this can lead to a couple of problems.

First problem: as you know, if someone is overworked they are more likely to make mistakes. Your Fixer is no exception. The more often it has to do its job, the greater the chance of it making a mistake — such as going back to its old methods and using nicotine to cheer you up.

Second problem: if your Fixer gets triggered a lot, it might conclude that the new methods (that you have asked it to use) aren't working very well. As a result, it might lose faith in these new methods and start trying nicotine again.

For these reasons, *you want to give your Fixer as little work to do as possible*. Since your Fixer springs into action whenever you feel any negative emotion, it's a good idea to have as few negative thoughts and feelings as possible. In short:

- Negativity leads back to smoking slavery (or at least increases the risk).
- Positivity leads forward to a life free from smoking.

Obviously, unless you live a very strange life, you can't feel positive about everything, all the time. Life has its annoyances and frustrations — there's a wasp for every picnic, so to speak. The point is to *try* to stay as positive as you can, as often as you can, to give your Fixer as little work to do as possible. One thing that will help a great deal is to use positive language.

Positive Language

You can't control everything in life and bad stuff happens. What you *can* control is the language you use and how you express yourself. In order to stay great and not start smoking again, I strongly recommend that you start expressing yourself in positive terms.

It's not hard to get the hang of doing this. You just have to think about things in a slightly different way. This applies to your thoughts and *internal* monologue as well as whatever you say to other people. For example, don't refer to yourself in a negative way. Be a good friend to yourself and always look for the positive spin. Here are some examples.

Negative: "I'm hopeless at this."

Positive: "I might not be great at this yet, but I'm doing my best to learn and getting better all the time."

Negative: "I really messed that up."

Positive: "I tried my best but I was unlucky. It was a difficult situation and didn't turn out the way I'd hoped. We all know life has its ups and downs and not every day is a trophy day. I'll learn from this and do better next time."

You get the idea? Of course, you have to take responsibility for your actions. Nonetheless, learn to be less self-critical and more forgiving. Go easy on the self-blame and learn the art of loving yourself, respecting yourself and referring to yourself in a positive way.

No-No To 'Stop-Go'

Most smokers are familiar with the notion of 'Stop-Go' smoking. You manage to quit for a while but then you go back to it, then quit again but then start once more. As many smokers have said, "Giving up smoking is easy... I do it two or three times a year."

This is unsurprising given that many people who try to give up smoking aren't given good information about how to do it. They use an ineffective approach, almost always relying on willpower (which doesn't work), so of course they sooner or later go back to smoking again. In this book, I am *not* suggesting you rely on willpower so I doubt you'll have this 'Stop-Go' problem. I have given you the tools you need to get the job done properly, once and for all.

Nonetheless, once you have quit smoking, don't take it for granted that you'll never use nicotine again. Sustain and nourish your relationship with your Fixer. It has learned new ways to keep you happy whenever necessary. Help it get used to these new strategies and thank it when it looks after you the way you *want* to be looked after.

Every day, enjoy being free from addiction knowing you're taking responsibility for yourself and looking after your health as best you can.

Mind And Body

After you have quit smoking, it might take a while for your *mind* to catch up with your *body*.

Suppose you were a smoker for ten years before you quit. For those ten years, your attitudes, behaviours and choices were those of a smoker who regularly used nicotine to achieve changes in your emotional state. It's understandable if your mind takes a while to absorb the changes and get used to your new way of living.

Sustaining a good relationship with your Fixer is an important part of this. In addition, recognise that this is *an ongoing process*. Give your mind time to catch up and be aware of all the choices and decisions you make. Be ready to stop yourself from time to time and say, "Ah, wait a minute. That thought or impulse I've just had is a *relic* from the old days. It's a negative pattern that doesn't really fit how I live my life now. I have better options these days and should update my ideas and behaviour accordingly."

Giving up smoking isn't just about working with your body. Work with your mind as well. They come as a package!

You're Free, Not Deprived

Once you've quit smoking, never succumb to the delusion that you are being *deprived* of anything or that you are no longer *allowed* to have a cigarette. These are both negative feelings that can lead back to addictive behaviour.

When someone says you can't have something, it's natural to feel resentment. This intensifies your desire to get what you've been told you can't have — especially if it's something you see lots of other people (apparently) enjoying. Any negative feelings of being deprived will prompt your Fixer to try to make sure that you, too, enjoy whatever 'treat' is being considered.

How can you avoid these feelings and problems? Well, the *words* you use can make a big difference to how you feel. Consider these two ways of expressing yourself:

(1) "I *can't have* cigarettes. I'm *not allowed* to have them now. I have to *deny* myself that pleasure — even though I can see lots of other people smoking and they look perfectly okay."

(2) "I can have all the cigarettes I want. The amount I want is precisely 'none' because I know that, despite the way nicotine is advertised, it isn't my friend. It's a carcinogenic and powerfully addictive substance that hurts my body and would almost certainly lead to some very serious and unpleasant health problems. I'd rather have nothing to do with smoking and all its very unfortunate consequences."

The first version is full of alarming words and phrases: 'can't have', 'not allowed', 'deny'. These are likely to trigger a sense of protest that can lead to a sense of 'rebellion' and a desire to have something purely to demonstrate that you refuse to be imprisoned by rules.

The second option lacks any trace of this negativity. It doesn't convey any sense of denial or deprivation. You have all the choices, all the power, all the control. You choose to use your power to look after yourself. You are in charge and prefer to look after your health instead of using a substance that you don't need and that you know greatly increases your chances of suffering nasty things like cancer.

You're not a slave to a substance that will hurt you. You are *free* from it and all of its consequences.

You're not deprived. You're *powerful* and use your power to look after yourself.

Feedback Loops

When it comes to giving up smoking for good and staying great, one final idea you might like is that of *feedback loops.*

Addictions involve negative feedback loops. Before I discovered how to quit smoking, I was unhappy about the cost, the effects on my health and how I seemed unable to escape the addiction. Because I was unhappy, my Fixer tried to cheer me up using whatever methods it felt would work, which of course included smoking! This lifted my mood for a short time but later on I felt bad because I was still a smoker. It was a perfect example of a vicious circle or a negative feedback loop.

Once I had quit smoking, I noticed a range of benefits. It felt good to know I'd finally taken responsibility for my health and was saving money. I also appreciated the fact that life was a little simpler because I was no longer constantly figuring out how to maintain my supply of cigarettes. These good feelings encouraged me to carry on, day by day, living as a non-smoker. The longer I went without tobacco, the easier it became and the more positive I felt about my freedom from addiction. These good feelings helped me to remain free of any inclination to smoke. This is an example of a positive feedback loop.

Beware negative feedback loops. They do not, and cannot, lead to anywhere good.

Build positive feedback loops into your life. They help you continue to live your life with freedom, choice and control.

Progress Check

In Step 4, 'Staying Great', we considered some aspects of living the rest of your life as a non-smoker and how to make sure you never start smoking again.

You will find some more information in Part 2: 'More About Staying Great' and 'More About Positive Attitudes'.

This brings Part One to an end. You have all the information and tools you need to stop smoking forever. What's more, you know how to do it the easy-ish way.

Part Two: Additional Information

In Part Two, I want to offer a lot of additional details and information that you might find useful and interesting. Enjoy whichever sections happen to interest you and ignore the rest.

I didn't put all this material earlier in the book because I wanted to keep Part One as short and simple as possible.

> ### Important - Please Read!
> I have no medical or therapeutic qualifications.
>
> If you are going to make any significant changes in your life, you should first go to see your doctor or physician. Discuss the changes you intend to make and take their advice.
>
> I do not accept responsibility for any aspect of your health. You should not regard anything in this book as medical advice. The contents of this book are only offered as personal testimony, opinion and information. I do not promise or guarantee any specific results or outcome. If you take any of my advice, you do so entirely at your risk and on the basis that every individual is different so results may vary.

The Ideas This Book Is Based On

It's very easy for a book like this to be misunderstood or for people to misconstrue my motives for writing it. This being the case, let me clearly state the two ideas this book is based on:

- Smoking hurts health.

- Addiction bad, freedom good.

Smoking Hurts Health

We all know that when it comes to health, there are no guarantees or certainties. Some people, though they try their best to live very healthy lives, get a non-preventable illness anyway. Others do all the 'bad' unhealthy things and live hale and hearty lives, still wrestling tigers at 90. Luck is a factor and is, by definition, not a predictable quality.

Statistical flukes at either end of the scale don't tell us much. The way we figure out what's most *likely* to promote good health is to look at the data from large numbers of people over long periods of time. This is how we know that if you smoke, you greatly increase the chances that you'll suffer from something horrible, disgusting and painful. Let's consider a few examples.

According to the World Health Organisation, tobacco smoke and/or nicotine greatly increases your risk of lung cancer, oral cancer and large number of other cancers, heart attack, stroke and several cardiovascular diseases, asthma, obstructive pulmonary disease, tuberculosis, Type 2 diabetes and dementia. That's just the start of a very long and relentlessly grim list. Experiencing any of these conditions or diseases won't be nice for you or for anyone who cares about you.

In fact, if you go to the WHO website, you can download a document called 'The Tobacco Body', which summarises all the nasty consequences of smoking or using nicotine on a single page. It features one of the most (intentionally) gruesome and repulsive graphics you'll ever see: a representation of a single body affected by all the possible consequences of smoking. It looks like the poster for a particularly grotesque horror movie.

Smoking hurts health. When you quit smoking, you give yourself the best possible chance of staying healthy for as long as you can. I think this sounds like a good idea. What's more, I think you deserve this and that you're worth it.

Addiction Bad, Freedom Good

Addiction is the opposite of freedom, choice and control.

Any addiction is bad. Serious addiction can ruin the life of both the addict and their loved ones and friends.

Freedom, choice and control are good.

There is no upside to being addicted. There is no downside to freedom.

Anyone who uses tobacco or nicotine on a regular basis has some type of addiction. It may be mild or strong but the addiction is always there. My aim is to help as many people as I can to escape the chains of addiction and enjoy freedom, choice and control instead.

The less addiction there is in the world, the better for us all.

That's the lot. Those are the two ideas this book is based on.

Ideas This Book Is Not Based On

Just for the record, I haven't written this book because I want to tell anyone what to do. I have no interest in trying to make everyone the same or taking away people's simple pleasures in life. I am neither a puritan nor a 'killjoy' (as anyone who knows me will readily confirm).

I am not preaching or pretending to be pious, perfect or better than anyone else. Nothing in this book is about trying to take away anyone's right to enjoy a legal drug. I do understand that how you choose to live your life is up to you, not up to me. I am well aware of this.

If you nonchalantly say you are happy to 'take your chances' with your health, you are entitled to do so. Also, it's true that doctors don't know everything and statistics can be misleading. I accept that you can probably think of someone — a friend or elderly relative — who smokes a lot and never seems to have any problems.

These are all 'straw man' arguments and objections. They have nothing to do with this book or my motives for writing it.

More About The Want Fix

In Step 2, 'Change Your Mind', I explained the Want Fix technique — how to change what you feel you want. Here's some more information about it.

I didn't invent the Want Fix. It's basically just my name for a therapeutic technique called Parts Integration, which has been around for a while. It's derived from the work of American therapist Virginia Satir, a pioneer in the field of family therapy. Even though it's far from new, I get the impression that very few people have ever heard of Parts Integration. Even some professional therapists are apparently unaware of it.

Most of what I know about Parts Integration comes from my friend James Mallinson, a highly experienced hypnotherapist who runs the 'Fix My Mind' clinic. He is a truly wonderful person to talk to regarding all aspects of the mind and how it works.

James told me that Parts Integration is based on the idea that your unconscious has good intentions that are themselves unconscious unless you become aware of them. As an individual, you create parts of yourself that reside within your own internal ecosystem. In moments of emotional significance, you may create a part such as an 'addict' whose role is to make you feel better. To take a common example, it might use sugar as a quick way to make you feel good.

Unfortunately, your *behaviour* may be completely counter to your *intention*, which can create conflict. For example, a smoker might say, "Part of me hates smoking but part of me likes it". The therapist seeks to neutralise this type of conflict. There are several ways to do this but the basic principle is to help the patient become aware of the two parts and the nature of the conflict, and to focus on the *ultimate* intention (feeling as good as possible, as often as possible).

The therapist and patient, working together, can encourage the 'addict' to give up one behaviour (that doesn't serve the ultimate intention very well) and replace it with one that's more likely to be successful. In effect, the patient manages to create a new part that integrates the parts that were previously separate and in conflict.

If ever you want to work with a trained, professional therapist, James is the one I recommend. He's very knowledgeable, experienced and approachable.

More About Meditation

In Step 2, 'Change Your Mind', I explained that the Want Fix starts with meditation. Here's a bit more information if you want it.

Meditation is very good for your physical, mental and emotional health. It's free and you can do it just about anywhere. You don't need any special equipment and there's no need to tie yourself in knots, embrace strange beliefs or make yourself uncomfortable. I'm going to briefly describe the type of meditation I use, just in case it's of interest.

1. Choose a time when there are as few distractions as possible. I like incense so I generally light some before I start but that's optional. Sit anywhere you feel comfortable — on a favourite chair, on the edge of your bed, in your garden, on the beach... wherever you like.

2. Close your eyes and relax as much as you can. Just focus on your own breathing for a while.

3. Breathe in slowly, completely filling your lungs, while you count from 1 to 4. You need a tactile way to count. I rest my hands on my thighs and count by very lightly tapping my forefinger on my thigh.

4. Hold your breath for a count of 7.

5. Breathe out slowly and evenly for a count of 8. Try to exhale completely, so that by the time you get to 8 you have expelled all the air from your lungs.

6. Repeat this 4-7-8 cycle a few times. You might like to see how far you can slow down this cycle, reaching the point where you feel very relaxed and mellow.

7. Having done a few 4-7-8 cycles, and achieved a deep state of relaxation, allow yourself to breathe normally without counting, though still in a very slow, even and relaxed way.

8. You can now use your meditation time in any way that you want. You can go through affirmations about your life, your goals, the person you want to be or anything else. You can work on your self-confidence, visualise the success you want to achieve or communicate with your Fixer and go over your Want Fix. Use the time as you wish.

9. When you're ready to end the session, go through a few more cycles of 4-7-8 breathing then slowly open your eyes and re-engage with the world around you.

There are many styles of meditation. If you don't like the one that I've described, explore other approaches until you find one that you do like. You can find a local teacher, read about meditation online, watch video tutorials or ask friends.

How long should you meditate for and how often? Whatever works best for you. I generally enjoy four or five sessions per week. I set the timer on my phone and generally meditate for about 15 minutes per session. I take more time if I feel like it and less time if I'm in a bit of a time crush and have discovered, rather annoyingly, that the day that has been delivered isn't long enough to fit in all the things I need to do in it, which is clearly not my fault. I also have short 'top up' sessions lasting just a few minutes whenever I feel like it.

I learned about the 4-7-8 breathing technique from a video featuring the consistently wonderful Dr. Andrew Weil, who offers plenty of excellent advice on a broad range of health subjects. You should check out his work online.

You may also like to read a delightful book by Dan Harris called '10% Happier', which celebrates the joys of meditation. It has an excellent subtitle: 'How I Tamed the Voice in My Head, Reduced Stress Without Losing My Edge and Found Self-Help That Actually Works — A True Story'. It's an excellent, easy-to-read book and, among other things, a wonderful cautionary tale for anyone who thinks drugs are either fun or a good way to cope with a high pressure job.

More About Staying Great

For this section, let's assume that all your *medical* needs, as determined by your doctor or a qualified medical professional, are taken care of. Also, that you have used the information in Part One to quit smoking.

If you want a few ideas and suggestions from me about staying great and feeling as good as you can, as often as you can, here they are. My first piece of advice would be this: when it comes to health and well-being, always consider *lifestyle* before *medication*. You have probably been conditioned to think that feeling better usually involves getting a pill, a tablet, a tonic, a supplement or something else that offers a 'quick fix' solution. No effort, no change to your lifestyle — just swallow something and all will be well. There are even some (not all) family doctors who propagate this attitude, seldom if ever discussing lifestyle with their patients and instead just prescribing yet another drug.

I acknowledge there are times when you *do* need a drug or some type of medication. Reread the first paragraph on this page. I'm saying that if you want to enjoy the best and healthiest life you can, *outside* of your immediate medical needs, changing your lifestyle is a better bet, and less expensive, than looking for pills and supplements.

My next suggestion would be to always pay attention to your MEDS: meditation, exercise, diet and sleep. Meditate a few times a week. It's deeply enjoyable and very good for your mental and emotional health. Take regular exercise, and keep to a healthy, nutritious and enjoyable diet. Understand that sleep is incredibly important for your health and try to make sure you get enough of it. (If you are the parent of young children, I will understand if, at this point, you respond with a hollow laugh of despair.)

Find an activity that provides a pleasant antidote to stress (other than regular exercise) and that you can turn to more or less whenever you want to. You want something that seems to light up a separate set of mental circuits and put you into a calm frame of mind. Ideally, find something active rather than just passively staring at a screen. For example, you could do some type of arts and crafts or work on something creative.

I *love* playing my guitar which, despite the fact that I'm not very good, is a very calming, soothing way to take a break from work or change my mood. Whenever I pick up my guitar and doodle for a while, it puts my mind into 'calm, restful and playful' mode. Find your own equivalent and make it your instant mind refuge that you turn to whenever you feel like it.

Explore and enjoy nature as far as possible. I don't know what you've got near you: forests and woodlands, parks and meadows, beaches and lakes or maybe hills and mountains. Whatever's available, immerse yourself in the natural world as often as you can. Apart from all the other benefits, you'll see some beautiful sights that gladden your spirit. When Nature shows off, as she is often happy to do, there's very little that can compare — and it's a free show.

Maintain good relationships in your life. Your partner, family, friends and colleagues are all important. Nourish and sustain the good relationships and distance yourself from the toxic ones. As the saying goes, 'The way to have a good friend is to *be* a good friend'. Human warmth and contact is incredibly healing and therapeutic. Many of life's problems can be alleviated, or at least put into perspective, by a good chat over a cup of tea or coffee. If you can't chat to someone in real life, do it online.

Hugs and cuddles are also good for your health and well-being, as is fulfilling and enjoyable sex. If you haven't read 'The Joy Of Sex' by Alex Comfort, I suggest you do so. It's a wonderful book and delightful to read. Men are very reluctant to admit they'd like a hug or a cuddle because the vocabulary doesn't sound 'masculine' enough. This is a shame and it's something that we men really need to get over.

Make sure there is laughter in your life. If you have a good sense of humour, share it. If you don't, learn to cultivate one. Humour is a wonderful way to connect with people and to smooth out some of life's rough edges. Someone once said, 'The shortest distance between two people is a smile'. Have some playfulness in your life too. Play is important. Many creative people will tell you that they get some of their best ideas just from playing, improvising and having fun.

Do some charitable work. I don't mean just giving money, although that's a good idea as well. I mean actually give your time and effort to a worthwhile cause and doing some voluntary work. Even a few hours spent helping people less fortunate than yourself will give you a much healthier perspective on life.

Explore what's meant by critical thinking. Learn what does, and does not, constitute good evidence and good reasoning. Have lots of good thinking tools in your mental toolbox and know how to avoid fallacious reasoning. Find out what people mean when they talk about 'Straw man' arguments, circular reasoning, 'correlation is not causation' and so on. Critical thinking skills, as well as helping you to save time and money, are good for your mental and emotional health. They also help you to overcome brainwashing, which helps you to enjoy freedom, choice and control.

Finally, I would encourage you to check out the work of health and diet expert Dr. Pamela Popper. She consistently and brilliantly argues the point that, when it comes to health and well-being, we should all think less about medication and more about positive lifestyle changes.

Pamela has written many popular books and has also posted numerous excellent videos online. Take a look at some of them. She covers such a broad range of subjects that I'm sure you'll be able to find several that interest you or that seem directly relevant to your own health and well-being. You may also be pleasantly surprised — she's very good at dismantling a lot of health and fitness mythology and correcting common misapprehensions.

Those are my ideas and suggestions for feeling as good as you can, as often as you can. You might also enjoy the next section which is all about positive attitudes.

NICOTINE I NOT NICE

More About Positive Attitudes

In Step 4, 'Stay Great', I mentioned the importance of maintaining a positive attitude as far as you can. When you experience negative thoughts and feelings, your Fixer springs into action to fix your mood. The more *often* this happens, the greater the chance of two problems.

First problem: your Fixer might make a mistake and use nicotine to make you happy rather than some other, non-harmful way. Second problem: your Fixer might lose faith in the new methods you have asked it to use and revert to its old repertoire.

To put this in very simplified terms:

- Negative leads back to nicotine.
- Positive leads forward to healthy.

It's therefore a good idea to avoid negative feelings as far as possible. Of course, staying positive is easier said than done. Here are some additional notes that will help.

Positive Language, Not Poison Language

In Step 4, I gave examples of using positive language when you refer to yourself, like this:

Negative: "I'm hopeless at this."

Positive: "I might not be great at this yet, but I'm learning really well and getting better all the time."

Expressing negative things about yourself, even in fun, leads to negative attitudes and behaviour. You might think it goes like this:

"I am a loser so I tend to refer to myself as a loser (because I'm just being honest about it)."

In fact, it actually works the other way round:

"Because I *hear* myself say I'm a loser, I've started to *behave* the way I'd expect a loser to behave."

When your *words* stay positive, *you* stay positive. So there's less work for your Fixer to do, so less chance of reverting to 'smoking' mode.

Positive Language > Positive Expectations

You can also use positive language to shape your *expectations*. For example, suppose you are starting a new job. You could say this:

> "I'm starting my new job tomorrow. I expect I'll find it pretty tough. I don't know if I'll manage it, to be honest."

By describing it to yourself in these terms, you are *conditioning* yourself to find it difficult. This works better:

> "I'm starting my new job tomorrow. It's an exciting challenge and I'm keen to see how it goes. I expect I'll do pretty well so long as I just take it a step at a time and give myself time to settle in. I'll make a few mistakes at first but that's all right. I'm just going to take it at my own pace."

This creates the expectation that you're going to find your new challenge interesting and that you'll enjoy it. This, in turn, affects your attitude and your experience of trying this new route.

It's the same with almost any other aspect of your life. Routinely adopting positive language will help you in countless ways. Conversely, negative language will never help anything at all. Some people refer to this as the difference between a *threat* mentality and a *challenge* mentality. Threats are scary and negative. Challenges are fun, exciting and stimulating.

ABC: Attitude > Behaviour > Consequences

Another way to think about the use of positive language is to remember 'ABC': Attitude shapes Behaviour which shapes Consequences.

This applies to any challenge: doing a bit more exercise, preparing for an exam or job interview, learning a new skill, improving a relationship or anything else.

If you have a positive attitude, this fosters positive behaviour: preparing properly, doing the work, taking all the best advice you can, planning your time and strategy and generally stacking the odds in your favour. This significantly increases the chances of good results and consequences.

If you have a negative attitude, the opposite is true. If you convince yourself from the start that you'll fail, you won't prepare well or devote much time to the project, which of course makes it likely you *will* fail. Every negative attitude becomes a self-fulfilling prophecy.

Self-Doubt No, Self-Great Yes

This section is about the importance of staying positive so you give your Fixer as little work to do as possible. We've just looked at the importance of positive *language*. Here's another tip: never have any self-doubt.

There are four main sources of self-doubt: yourself, other people, the outside world and the fear of failure. Here are some strategies for dealing with all of these.

Self-Doubt From You

I'm sure you can remember a time when you tried to do something and didn't do it very well. Maybe you were able to just shrug it off. Then again, maybe the experience got stored away inside you as a negative message that basically says, "I'm no good."

What's the fix?

To start with, it's not your job to be perfect all the time. When you came into this world, you never signed anything promising to be flawless. Consider this general plan for life:

- Strive to fulfil your potential, whatever it happens to be, and to help others do the same.

- Don't hurt yourself or anyone else. This involves being fair, honest and kind.

- Always do the best you can with what you have at the time.

If you can honestly say you're living by these principles, you're golden. Nobody can ask anything more of you.

The part about fulfilling your potential is interesting. It will involve trial and error, learning from experience as you go along. Your job is to strive and learn, doing the best you can with what you've got. This is all you can do. When your efforts turn out well, celebrate! When they don't, learn the lessons that will enable you to do better next time. Everything you try leads either to success or learning — both of which are welcome aspects of your journey.

This isn't always easy. Some 'learning experiences' can be difficult to deal with. We all take some hard punches from time to time and I've had my share, believe me! All I'm suggesting is that, as far as you can, take the positive view and avoid giving in to self-doubt.

Self-Doubt From Others

From time to time in life, you have to deal with negativity from other people: unkind words, harsh judgments and so on. It's not always easy to deal with but you must never let it lead to self-doubt.

What's the fix?

Whenever you face criticism, I have a suggestion. Ask yourself if it passes two tests:

> (1) Is it informed? Does this person actually know what they are talking about?

> (2) Is it constructive? Is this person offering criticism in order to help you to achieve better results?

If the criticism passes these two tests, you should welcome it because it's *really* useful. Listen well, take notes and benefit as much as you can from it.

If the criticism fails either or both of these tests, it is literally useless. You don't have to respond in an angry or defensive way. Just *peacefully* ignore it on the basis that there's nothing else you *can* do with it.

One more way to insulate yourself from useless criticism (as opposed to the informed and constructive type) is to watch Brené Brown giving her talk about 'The Man In The Arena'. You can find it online and it's absolutely superb.

Another good tip is to realise that no matter what you do, you can't please all the people, all the time. For example, I know a classically trained musician who hates the music of Mozart. Imagine that — even a creative genius like Mozart can't please everyone! Whenever someone is disparaging about your work, congratulate yourself on being in the same situation as Mozart. The same point is beautifully expressed by this quote from Abraham Lincoln, which I love:

> "If I were to try to read, much less answer, all the attacks made on me, this shop might as well be closed for any other business. I do the very best I know how — the very best I can, and I mean to keep on doing so until the end. If the end brings me out all right, what is said against me won't amount to anything. If the end brings me out wrong, ten angels swearing I was right would make no difference."

Doesn't that just say it all?

Self-Doubt From The Outside World

So far, we've looked at self-doubt that can come from yourself or from other people. The world at large can also be an abundant source of self-doubt, particularly the mass media and social media.

We hear a lot these days about young, impressionable women seeing pictures of supermodels in magazines and feeling inadequate by comparison. Page after page of advertising rams home the same message: "You aren't quite good enough the way you are — but if you buy this make-up, maybe you will be."

It's not just young, impressionable women who suffer from this kind of toxic propaganda. No matter who you are, the world gives you plenty of opportunities to feel that you're not quite good enough. The rise of social media has made things even worse, giving you more chances than ever to decide that everyone else is doing better than you are and you'll never catch up.

What's the fix?

If you're striving to do the best you can with what you've got, then you're immune from criticism. You can't ask any more of yourself and neither can anyone else. It's fine to have goals and aspirations, so long as they come from you and what you feel you want to achieve. Don't let the media and advertisers dictate what you *should* want or what shape your aspirations *ought* to take. Their interests are not your interests. You are the expert on the subject of you.

Remember that there's no need to compare yourself to anyone or anything else — either in real life or online. You can't be anyone else and no one else can be you. Social media can be fun and useful but be careful. As the popular advice goes, 'Don't compare someone else's highlights reel with your everyday life'. I've also heard this expressed as, 'Don't compare your inside to someone else's outside'.

Finally, beware the dangers of selectivity. If you're selective enough, a chess board only has white squares on it (or black ones). It's the same with your experiences in life and your self-esteem. You can choose to see *only* the things you get right and your good points or to see only the opposite. It's healthier to see the whole picture.

Be a friend to yourself and pay *more* attention to the positives than the negatives. It's good to be aware of a few aspects of your life where you could do better. At the same time, make sure you pay even *more* attention to the things you do well, the things you've got right so far and your likeable qualities.

Self-Doubt From Fear Of Failure

We've looked at three potential sources of negativity: yourself, other people and the outside world. The fourth most common source of self-doubt is the fear of failure.

The word 'fail' has lots of negative connotations. It's natural to think that if you fail then something will go wrong or you'll be mocked or criticised. These worries can lead you to feel that it's safer to do nothing than to risk failing. Of course, if you do nothing then you'll never taste success either. You may be familiar with the old saying: 'The person who never made a mistake never made anything'.

What's the fix?

Failure isn't something to worry or feel bad about. It's just one part of your growth and learning. In fact, some people say the word 'FAIL' stands for 'First Adventure In Learning'. To fail is to learn what doesn't work or isn't the right path to whatever you're trying to achieve. This puts you in a much better position to try again.

When you were just a baby, you couldn't even walk. You kept trying and trying, always stumbling and falling over. Your parents encouraged you to keep trying and praised every small sign of improvement. In the end, after lots of failures, you gradually got the hang of it. You never felt bad or self-conscious about it. Today, you're so used to walking that you take it for granted. 'Failing' is the name we give to the process of learning.

If you're interested in this subject, I highly recommend you read 'Black Box Thinking' by Matthew Syed. This fascinating and highly readable book is about why we should change our attitude towards so-called 'failure'. As Syed demonstrates with persuasive clarity, the process of 'failing' and learning what *doesn't* work is tremendously important. In many cases, it's the only way to find out what *does* work. Even if you just read the first chapter of this mind-opening book, it will transform the way you feel about failure.

You may also want to check out the work of Brené Brown, whom I've already mentioned once in this chapter. She's a wonderful speaker and writer who, among other subjects, addresses various aspects of what is often commonly referred to as failure. Check out some of her talks and articles. She came up with one of my favourite quotations: "You're imperfect, and you're wired for struggle, but you are worthy of love and belonging."

I couldn't agree more!

Two Bits Of Psychology

This section is all about staying great. The point is to have as few negative emotions as possible so you minimise the amount of work your Fixer has to do. To this end, here are a couple of notes about psychology you might find useful.

Critical People

Some people take great delight in criticising others, usually to feel better about themselves. Consider someone who says, "There are lots of idiot drivers on the roads these days." In saying this, the speaker is implying that they themselves are *not* one of the idiots and are, in fact, a *good* driver. By faulting others, they drape themselves in (implied) virtue.

If you have to deal with people like this, realise that maybe it's just what they need to do at the time. Maybe they aren't getting the credit, respect or gratification they want from anywhere else so they're trying to create it for themselves. Maybe they don't feel loved or appreciated, or they're going through a difficult time. Never worry about this kind of criticism. It's just how some people give themselves an ego cuddle. If you get to know them better, maybe you can help them to find other ways to feel good about themselves *without* feeling the need to denigrate others.

Angry People

Angry people often provoke negative feelings. When someone behaves angrily towards you, this can easily spur your Fixer into action.

Here's what you need to know: *anger is the sound of emotional frustration*. Consider a newborn baby in its cot. It is basically helpless and lacks any way to feed itself or take care of its needs. The one thing it *can* do is make a loud noise to get attention. This is how the baby gets fed, changed and comforted. As people grow older they acquire greater independence and learn more ways of satisfying their own needs.

Life presents problems and challenges and we all respond as best we know how. When people start to run out of steps, and can't think of a way to deal with their problems, they can respond in various ways. Some just give up, withdraw and become wrapped in feelings of despair. Others choose to make a loud noise, just like the baby in its cot. They are signalling that they have run out of steps, or fear they soon will, and make a loud noise (express anger) as a strategy of last resort. It worked when they were a baby and, in lieu of better options, they figure they have nothing to lose by trying it again.

When you're dealing with an angry person, try to be patient and understanding. Life can be hard and people sometimes run out of coping strategies so they make a loud noise. Maybe it's what they need at the time in order to express their pain and thereby reduce it. So long as they don't hurt themselves or anyone else, you can allow for this up to a point.

Never let an angry outburst affect your perception of yourself. The other person's anger is a symptom of *their* problem, not yours. Bear in mind that anger can't last forever. Given the way people are wired up, it's just physically impossible. Anyone who tried to stay angry for a long time would just pass out.

If someone is in an angry state, don't try to communicate with them in a significant way. This won't work. A person can be angry or they can communicate successfully but they cannot do *both*. Play for time and wait for them to burn off the adrenalin and shift to a calmer frame of mind, which must happen eventually. Once they've reached this phase, *then* you can try to communicate with them. In some circumstances, perhaps you can help them to deal with whatever pain or fear they are feeling.

Handling Emotional Crunch Points

Let's say you have followed the steps in this book and things are going fairly well. Using the Want Fix and the PAT process, you are no longer a smoker. Great!

There's really only one thing that can seriously disrupt your progress: an emotional crunch point. You get some bad news, a relationship goes wrong, things get hard at work, you go through a big disappointment, somebody does something hurtful... and so on.

When you face an emotional crunch point, your Fixer swings into action and tries to make you feel better. The more upset, angry or hurt you feel, the more work your Fixer has to do. At first, it will try the new strategies that you have asked it to try. If these don't seem to work, your Fixer will go back to its old repertoire of methods, which of course include smoking.

So, how can you stay positive even when you're going through dark and difficult days? How can you prevent your Fixer feeling that it needs to resort to its old ideas? I don't want to sound glib about these types of problems. I can't provide all the answers and even if I could they would fall outside the scope of this book. What I can do is pass on a few strategies that might help.

Choose 'I Can'

You don't get to choose whether or not bad things happen in life.

You *do* get to choose how you respond to them.

Rather than focus on what you *can't* do anything about, focus on what you *can*. You have no control over what happened. You have *total control* over how you respond. The bad news, in itself, doesn't determine anything. How you respond is far more important.

Think about this scenario. A child is in a park enjoying an ice cream cone. She's careless for a moment and drops the ice cream. The child can't think of any way to undo this so she feels upset and cries. An adult wouldn't get upset because they can plan how to reach a better situation: go to the nearest vendor and buy another ice cream. The event itself isn't upsetting. Only the response ('Good thing gone, can't fix') is upsetting.

Adult problems feel very different to the ice cream example yet they work the same way. When you're going through difficult times, you can go into 'Good thing gone, can't fix' mode, getting upset and feeling sorry for yourself. Alternatively, you can think about the square you're on, the square you want to get to and how to get there. In other words, figure out how to get a new ice cream cone. It might be very challenging and difficult. Nevertheless, every step you take towards your goal will feel positive, good and fulfilling. You might like to remember this saying: 'It will be all right in the end. If it's not all right, it's not the end'.

You Are Not Your Feelings

When bad things happen, it's natural to feel sad, angry, upset and sorry for yourself. However, although you *experience* these feelings, they neither define nor limit you.

Your feelings are your awareness of your system processing emotional change and shock. You may have heard of the 'five stages of grief' as defined by Elizabeth Kubler-Ross: denial, anger, bargaining, depression and acceptance. When bad things happen, you may go through some or all of these feelings. Working through them in your own time won't be easy but neither will it last forever. You still get to choose your plan, your direction and your next few steps.

Recognising your perfectly valid feelings doesn't mean they *limit you*. A feeling is your awareness of change and a new situation. It is not a prison cell. You can still take steps to get to a better place.

Connect Not Reject

When bad things happen, it's understandable if you feel like being on your own for a while. However, solitude is bad medicine. As soon as you can, connect with someone and talk about what you're going through. Just talking and being listened to feels much better than being on your own.

There's no shame in reaching out to people for whatever help you need. You can reach out informally to your partner, family, friends and colleagues. Alternatively, you can reach out on a more formal basis to trained professionals such as a doctor, counsellor or therapist (either in real life or online).

It's *easy* to feel that you don't *want* to connect with anyone. Do it anyway. You will get *tremendous* therapeutic benefit just from talking about what's happened and being listened to. The person you're talking to doesn't have to offer suggestions or solutions (unless you're asking for specific, practical expertise). The important part is just that you express yourself and feel listened to. There are times when the best healing comes from *connection* rather than isolation.

The 'Treated Me Badly' Trap

A very common source of negative feelings is the notion that someone has 'treated you badly'. This is a very common refrain. "I thought we had a great relationship but he treated me badly." "I worked hard on that project with her but then she treated me badly." "I did a lot for that organisation but then they treated me badly."

This is a delusion. It can be *very* difficult to free yourself from this delusion. Letting go of it can be a tough, difficult fight. However, it's worth making the effort. You will avoid a lot of negative feelings and also avoid harbouring grudges.

Here's the reality. Everyone is striving for the same things: some happiness, contentment, fulfilment, gratification and success. Look up 'Maslow's hierarchy of needs' if you want a more detailed list. Everyone is doing the best they can, with what they have at the time, to obtain these things.

The 'what they have' part varies tremendously. Everyone has different strengths, talents, abilities and natural aptitudes. Some people get a great start in life, some don't. Some people enjoy more luck than others. Some understand why hard work, integrity, honesty, fairness, kindness and sharing matter. Other are never given this training or these values.

No one ever woke up one morning and thought, "Today, my plan is to treat [your name] badly." Whatever they did, they were just doing the best they could, with what they had at the time, to be as happy and content as they knew how to be. Maybe what they did was wrong in the moral, ethical or legal sense. If they did something that you would never do, because you have better values and principles, be glad you learned those values somewhere on your journey. They will serve you well.

Why is it important to realise all this and how does it help you to stay great? First, it's better to see reality than to labour under a delusion. If you try to figure out why someone 'treated you badly', you'll go crazy because you're trying to explain something that didn't happen. It's like trying to solve a puzzle that has no answer.

The second reason is that it stops you seeing yourself as 'the person that someone treated badly'. This casts you in the low status role of a victim. It's a toxic way to see yourself and gives rise to a lot of negative feelings. Never harm yourself in this way. Someone who behaves in what seems to be a shabby or destructive way is showing that they don't have the personal resources to do any better. This is *their* deficiency, not yours. They are the victim, not you.

Choose Your Comparisons

Here's another aspect of staying great: choose good comparisons.

In life, you can always choose your comparisons. If you compare your situation to an obviously better one, you will understandably tend to feel bad. Alternatively, if you compare it to one that would be much worse, you tend to feel good or at least okay. I suggest you choose the 'good / okay' option.

For example, you might see someone enjoy more luck or success than you even though you've worked harder and in some way deserve it more. However, you have to remember that there will be some people who feel exactly the same way about *you*. From *their* point of view, you've got what *they* feel they deserve to have.

Imagine someone having a good moan about some bad news they've received recently. It could be a work issue or about money, relationships or any one of a dozen other things. Someone else might rather unhelpfully say, "Stop feeling sorry for yourself. There are some people far worse off than you." This kind of comparison, apart from being crass, doesn't make sense. To say you can't feel bad because someone else is worse off than you is like saying you can't feel good because someone else is *better* off.

However, it does raise an interesting point. Many negative feelings arise from the fact that life can be very unfair. Next time you feel upset about life's unfairness, you might want to consider all the ways in which life's unfairness *works in your favour*. Some people in the world don't have clean water to drink. They don't think it's particularly fair. Some never get the chance to learn how to read. Again, they don't think there's anything very fair about it.

I'm not saying you can't feel sad, upset or hurt. Of course you can. However, it's worth thinking about the comparisons you choose to consider and the many ways in which life's unfairness works in your favour. This can help you to deal with bad news, process it and gradually get past it.

Reading This For Free?

Are you reading an illegal copy of this book? Hey, I understand. There's a lot of copying and 'piracy' around these days, especially on the internet.

The thing is, writing books and selling them is part of how I earn a living. Writing this book involved a lot of time and effort. I haven't stolen anything from you. Please don't steal from me.

You can put things right! You can go to my website, buy this book legitimately *and* check out the *free* downloads, discount deals, extra information and other products: www.ianrowlandtraining.com

Wouldn't that be a nicer thing to do?

— Ian

More About Benefits

You are probably well aware of the benefits of giving up smoking. However, I felt there would be no harm in adding a little reminder section in this book. Some of what follows is based on data that you can look up for yourself. It's quite interesting to spend some time browsing the World Health Organisation website (which has a very good search facility) or just looking online for 'Benefits of quitting smoking'.

Some of what follows is based on personal experience. I was a smoker, on and off, for about eighteen years. At one point I reached the dizzy heights of sixty cigarettes a day. Currently, I've been a non-smoker for over twenty years.

(Almost Certainly) Better Health

This is the benefit everyone knows about, so I won't dwell on it at great length.

In my free booklet, 'Let's End Addiction' (which is available from www.ianrowlandtraining.com), I mention some illuminating statistics. In 2017, for example, about 7 *million* people died from smoking tobacco while another 1.2 million people died prematurely from *second-hand* smoking.

Why did these 7 million people die? Because they saw a tube of paper stuffed with what we know to be carcinogenic chemicals and thought, "My best choice, right now, is to set fire to that and suck the fumes into my lungs. In fact, I think I'll do this several times a day." As a society, I think we can help one another to make better choices than this.

Europe has the highest proportion of tobacco use in the world (29% or 209 million people). The stats show that, in this region, tobacco causes almost *one in five* premature deaths from non-communicable diseases. In any country, or any region of the world, healthcare resources are finite. I think it would be a good idea to devote these resources to non-preventable conditions, that can affect anyone regardless of lifestyle, rather than preventable ones.

Of course, whenever people discuss the health implications of smoking, the same arguments and objections tend to surface. "It's my choice, I enjoy a smoke, you can't stop me and I'll take my chances." "My old gran smoked forty a day, lived to be a hundred and never had a day's illness in her life." "We've all got to go one way or another, I may as well enjoy myself while I'm here."

If you think any of these arguments sound convincing, then I have no way of reaching you or connecting with you. All I can do is invite you to learn about critical thinking and how to assess whether an argument actually makes sense or not. If you do, you'll realise that all of these objections are flawed. They are just the sound of your addiction trying to protect itself. They are also signs of successful brainwashing by the tobacco industry.

The fact is, if you carry on smoking, you *greatly* increase the chances that you'll die prematurely of something horrible, painful and disgusting, such as lung cancer, cardiovascular disease, obstructive pulmonary disease and so on. If you quit smoking, you greatly increase the chances that this will *not* happen.

Your call.

You Will Feel Better

When you quit smoking, you will feel better in several ways. In fact, you'll feel better in every way you can feel better. There's no upside to smoking and no downside to quitting.

You will, of course, feel better physically. When you smoke, your body has to do quite a lot of extra work to cope with the regular intake of smoke, tar, nicotine and all the other junk involved — such as constantly trying to detoxify your blood. When your body no longer has to do all this extra work, life starts to feel a lot simpler and easier. You will breathe more easily, of course, which in turn leads to lots of other benefits (such as enjoying more energy and better sleep).

You will also feel better *mentally* and *emotionally*. You'll be glad that you took responsibility for yourself and your health, decided to make a positive change in your life and achieved it. Well done you!

You will enjoy the fact that you decided not to be a puppet of the tobacco industry any more. You realised that you weren't getting a good deal: you give them money, they give you dangerously addictive chemicals that will almost certainly lead to painful, disgusting diseases that you will *not* enjoy and don't need to suffer.

You'll feel good about having broken out of your addiction prison and chosen freedom, choice and control instead.

Here's the short version: no-one has ever quit smoking and, once they've adjusted to life without tobacco, said they felt *worse*. They all say they feel better and are pleased they did it.

More Energy And Efficiency

When you stop smoking, you'll find you have a lot more energy than you did before. Of course you do.

Smoke from tobacco contains lots of nasty junk. If you're interested, search online for 'what's in tobacco smoke' (Wikipedia has a good page about it). The full list includes formaldehyde, carbon monoxide, hydrogen cyanide, benzene and lots of other stuff that only a chemistry teacher would know how to pronounce.

When you smoke, your lungs and kidneys have to filter out all this rubbish, which is a lot of work. When you stop smoking, your lungs can work the way they're meant to: taking in air, extracting oxygen and supplying it (via your bloodstream) to your entire body. When your lungs have an easier life, *you* have an easier life.

Having more energy means, in turn, that you can be more productive and get a lot more done.

Better Leisure Time

When I was a smoker, I felt that all enjoyable social occasions had to involve smoking. Did I enjoy myself? Sure. I was also damaging my lungs, ruining my health and wasting a lot of money (since smoking cigarettes is, quite literally, a case of money up in smoke). I also had the fuss of always making sure I had adequate supplies of cigarettes or knew where I could get some. These days, many public places also have restrictions on smoking indoors that smokers have to contend with.

These days, I know I can thoroughly enjoy myself, in any situation, without smoking anything. I don't have to worry about having my cigarettes with me or about the restrictions in public places. You will enjoy similar benefits too, freeing yourself from the notion that enjoying yourself must always involve addictive substances in general or nicotine in particular. This is very liberating!

Better Looks, Better Skin, Nicer Teeth

No matter who you are, the 'non-smoker' version looks better than the 'smoker' version. Smoking has bad effects on your skin, hair and teeth. If you're young, these effects may not be too noticeable since youth is a great concealer. As the years go by, the damaging effects of smoking will become more evident. You can see the evidence for yourself when you take a good look at older people who have smoked for a long time.

Whatever else you want to say about tobacco, it never enhanced anyone's physical appearance.

You may say you don't care much about your appearance. Maybe you think that in today's society we place too much emphasis on superficial looks. I agree, but let me mention two points.

One, your level of interest in your appearance, and how you come across to other people, may change once you quit smoking.

Two, the fact that the non-smoker version of you will look better isn't just about shallow, superficial judgments. When people can see that you take responsibility for your health, it tends to create a sense of respect and admiration. In addition, if they know you used to smoke, they'll admire you all the more for having dealt with the problem and changed your life for the better.

Higher Testosterone Levels

Here's a note for my male readers. There is some evidence to suggest that when you quit smoking, you will almost certainly boost your testosterone levels. You may or may not care about this. Nevertheless, I think most men, if told that their testosterone level was going to go one way or the other, would prefer 'up' to 'down'. Personally, I can't say I've noticed any difference, although these days I do eat lots of raw meat for breakfast and often wrestle grizzly bears for fun.

Less Smell, Less Waste

Nobody likes to mention this to smokers because it seems impolite, but your body, clothes, car and home all smell of stale cigarette smoke. Sorry, but it's true. This is not an appealing smell. When you quit smoking, the smell will gradually fade away leaving a nicer ambience.

You may also start to enjoy a cleaner environment with less waste. I once knew a co-worker who was a heavy smoker. The interior of his car was essentially a shrine to cigars and ash. The ashtray was constantly full to overflowing and the ashy residue seemed to get everywhere. I sometimes had to be a passenger in his car, which was horrible even though I myself was a smoker at the time.

Some smokers have homes that are similarly blighted by smoke, ash and smoking residue. When you quit, you'll appreciate having a nicer, cleaner, fresher environment. This is also much more enjoyable for visitors and passengers.

More Money

At the risk of stating the obvious, when you stop smoking you stop cremating money. This means you have more to spend on other things. Can you think of something better to spend your money on? Of course you can. The hard part would be to think of anything *worse*.

Most smokers, at some point, have calculated how much they spend in a year on cigarettes or whatever it is they smoke. At the time of writing this book, someone in the UK with a modest habit of ten cigarettes a day would be spending about £1940 per year on smoking. In the US it comes to about $1040 per year. That's a lot to spend on something you don't need that makes you smell bad and clogs up your lungs.

Imagine suddenly being given this extra money to do with as you wish *and* having healthier lungs and a cleaner home into the bargain!

You'll Be Calmer, Less Stressed

Smokers often claim that smoking helps them to relax and cope with stress. This isn't true. In fact, I'll re-write that a bit more accurately: smokers often repeat a lie, put out by tobacco companies, that smoking helps you to relax. The tobacco companies say the lines and the smoker is the sock puppet.

I'm going to deal with this in two parts. First of all, I want you to understand what stress actually is. Then we'll asses this rubbish about smoking being a good way to deal with it.

Whenever you notice something that might be dangerous, your brain sends a signal to your adrenal gland. This produces a burst of adrenalin, which stimulates your heart and lungs to work faster so you have more energy. In theory, this extra energy enables you to fight the dangerous thing or run away from it. This is known as your 'flight or fight' response. It works automatically and can save your life in a dangerous situation. There are two things to know about this response:

- It's only meant to be a quick fix. One adrenalin burst is fine. Lots of it in your bloodstream for a long time is bad for you.

- This system only works if you're fit.

Being 'fit' means *you can adjust your energy levels to fit the situation*. Imagine a scale from 1 to 20, and your normal, resting heartbeat and breathing level is about 10. If you're fit and you suddenly need more energy, your heart and lungs can start to work harder, processing more oxygen, pumping more blood around your body and getting energy to where it's needed *fast*. You might be able to go up to, say, level 16 or 17. Your body responds well to the demands placed on it.

If you're unfit, you can't do this. Your heart and lungs have only practised going up to 11 or maybe 12.

Fitness also helps you to *relax*. If you're fit and you don't need much energy at the moment, because you're just relaxing or sleeping, your heart and lungs can slow down to, say, level 3 or 4.

If you're unfit, you can't do this. Your heart and lungs don't have the same kind of range. They may only be able to slow down to about 7 or 8, so you don't get as much benefit from your rest and sleep as a fit person does.

What's this got to do with stress?

Suppose you feel worried or anxious about something: problems at work, money worries, relationship difficulties or whatever. Your brain responds to these things just as it would to a sign of physical danger. It triggers the adrenal gland, you get a shot of adrenalin and your heart and lungs try to speed up.

If you're fit, your heart and lungs can respond appropriately, working harder to deliver more energy. If you're not fit, your heart and lungs can't do this (or not much) so nothing much changes. Since the thing you're worried about is still there, your brain tries another shot of adrenalin. This also doesn't work, so it tries another.

As I've said, having lots of adrenalin in your system isn't good. It's like constantly trying to get a machine to go faster than it can. Eventually, something's got to give. This is what stress is: the persistent experience of trying to respond to an anxious situation and not being able to.

Stress is seriously bad stuff. There's no way to sugar coat this for you. It's linked to many forms of cancer and heart disease as well as asthma, breathing difficulties, gastrointestinal conditions, insomnia, depression, Alzheimer's and accelerated ageing. There are no positives associated with stress. None.

If you have good physical fitness, this combats stress in two ways. First, your heart and lungs can respond to bursts of adrenalin, working harder and burning off the extra energy your body is making available. Secondly, you get better at *relaxing* and not worrying so much. Fitness means less stress, which means less work for your Fixer to do in terms of trying to keep you feeling good.

There are some really good ways to deal with stress. They are powerful, they work really well and they cost little or nothing:

- Get fit. (I have a book called 'The Easy-ish Way To Get Fit And Lose Weight', end of advert).

- Learn to meditate well and often.

- Take some of the advice I mentioned earlier in the section entitled 'More About Staying Great'.

Now, what about this notion that smoking helps you to relax and to cope with stress? It's not true. I was once a smoker so I know this can *seem* quite a convincing illusion. When you feel stressed and light up a cigarette, that initial 'hit' of nicotine does feel, for a moment, as if it helps you to calm down and feel a little better.

Note that I say 'as if'. It's a comforting illusion but it's not the truth. Here's the truth. You can handle the truth.

(1) I've just explained the link between stress and fitness. Because smoking harms your lungs, it can only ever make you *less* fit, not more. The less fit you are, the less able you are to deal with stress.

(2) When you smoke, you pollute your body with toxic chemicals. Your body then has to do extra work to try to detoxify your body (for example, your kidneys have to work overtime to clean up your blood). This extra work places a strain on your body. The cumulative effect is like trying to keep an engine running all the time — eventually, something has to give. This doesn't help you to relax or to calm down.

(3) When I explained the PAT Process, I pointed out that the feeling of needing a cigarette is, in itself, a *stress* response. The receptors in your body are sending an 'alarm' signal just as they would if you weren't getting enough oxygen. Every time you experience this feeling, you are flooding your system with stress hormones such as cortisol. It's a really bad idea to be doing this several times a day, every day.

You know you don't actually need tobacco or nicotine to relax or to cope with stress. You know that millions of people, all over the world, manage to relax and deal with stressful situations without using tobacco.

You may argue that you lead a particularly stressful or difficult life. If this is the case, you have my sympathy. However, I guarantee there is someone, somewhere who is facing all the same challenges, or worse, and yet somehow gets by without tobacco or nicotine. They know that *not* smoking makes it *easier* to deal with stress, not harder.

We all know that life can be rough, tough and difficult to deal with. While I won't claim to have had the hardest life imaginable, I've had my share of tough times, dark days and bleak chapters. You don't need smoking to get through them. Smoking doesn't actually help. Smoking just does what it always does: it hurts. You know this is the case. It hurts your money, your lungs, your health, your fitness and your future. That's all it *can* do.

Don't mistake the momentary sensation of a nicotine 'hit' for something that actually helps you to lead a less stressful life.

The One Downside

Having listed the many benefits of quitting smoking, it's only fair to mention the downside. I do this in the interests of balance and of giving you the whole picture.

Here it is. Here's the one disadvantage of quitting smoking: you will need to become quite good at graciously accepting compliments.

You'll be receiving a lot of them! Everyone who knows that you used to smoke but have now quit for good will congratulate you and respect your achievement.

Overcoming Emotional Resistance

If you follow the four steps in Part One of this book, I hope you'll be able to quit smoking the *easy-ish* way. However, you might experience some *emotional* resistance to the idea of giving up tobacco for good. How can you deal with this?

Let's look at how emotional resistance arises. Imagine you have an important job that you enjoy and that you like to do well. You believe the best tool for the job is your hammer, which you have successfully used for a number of years. If you were asked *not* to use the hammer anymore, you'd feel anxious about not being able to do your job as well as you normally do.

It's the same with your Fixer. It has learned a number of ways to keep you happy (such as using nicotine). When you ask your Fixer to do things a different way, it can feel rather worried. You are asking it *not* to use a method it has learned to trust. Your Fixer's concern, which is understandable, gives rise to feelings of *emotional resistance*. It's what leads people to say things like this:

"It's my right to enjoy smoking if I want to."

"I don't get a lot of pleasure in life. Enjoying a relaxing cigarette now and again is one of the few pleasures I have left."

"Smoking helps me deal with stress and relax at the end of a hard day's work."

"Not everyone wants to be a holier-than-thou puritan smugly telling everyone else how to live their lives."

"Okay, so it's a bad habit. So what? I'm human. I'm not perfect. We all have our weaknesses and this is one of mine. Leave me alone."

"Stop going on about the health risks. We've all got to go sometime so I may as well enjoy myself while I'm here."

"I've tried to quit and I know I can't. I admit it — I'm addicted. That's all there is to it."

All these sentiments are the sound of your Fixer getting anxious. This is what gives rise to the irrational tone and 'straw man' arguments. It's quite a leap to accuse someone of being a 'puritan' just because they think it might be nice for you *not* to get lung cancer.

Reassuring Your Fixer

The way to address emotional resistance is to communicate with your Fixer and address its concerns. Make it clear that you acknowledge all the great work it does and the excellent results it achieves, and that you are thankful. In addition, be clear that you *do* want it to carry on doing its brilliant work.

The only difference is that you're asking it to use methods that will work even *better* than the ones it has been using so far. The old methods might seem to work but they only deliver *fake* happiness for a *short* time. Better strategies help you to experience *real* happiness and contentment more or less *all* the time.

Put simply: make it clear you're not stopping your Fixer from doing its job. You're helping it to do its job *even more successfully than ever*. You are not just taking away the hammer. You are pointing out that the hammer doesn't really work as well as your Fixer thinks it does. You are giving your Fixer new and better tools so it can do its job even more successfully.

When you maintain your relationship with your Fixer, be ready to address these feelings of resistance whenever they arise. If you need to repeat your explanations, do so.

Freedom And The Right To Smoke

While we're here, I just want to add a short note about the 'right to smoke' argument. It's one I've come across many times in the twenty years since I stopped smoking and, to be honest, I'm surprised it gets recycled as often as it does. It is transparently absurd to argue for the freedom to be a slave — in this case, a slave of the tobacco companies that want to profit from your addiction.

I understand that many people have strong feelings about issues of personal liberty and individual freedom. These are important subjects. Here's the truth: if you are addicted to nicotine or anything else then you have *less* freedom, not more. Addiction is the *opposite* of freedom, choice and control. I'm all in favour of freedom. I'm against the chains of addiction and the prisons of dependency.

If you feel that personal freedom is important to you, then you and I are on the same page. I respect your views and will support you all the way. This is why I think you should pursue freedom from the tobacco companies, their products, what they want you to think and what they want you to say.

Some people say, "I want to be free to enjoy using tobacco".

Here's what they are really saying:

> "I want to be free to be a slave of the tobacco companies.
>
> I welcome their chains around my mind, making me believe what they want me to believe: that smoking is enjoyable and helps me to cope with life.
>
> I welcome their chains around my speech, making me say what they want me to say.
>
> I welcome their chains around my wallet or purse, making me give them money in return for some toxic chemicals that will eventually hurt me.
>
> I welcome their chains around my body, my lungs and my blood, making me dependent on their products.
>
> I welcome their chains around my life."

This doesn't sound much like freedom to me. If you really want freedom, tell the tobacco companies to get lost. Tell them you're choosing freedom and refuse to be their slave any longer. They are powerless to stop you walking away forever.

Why Willpower Isn't The Answer

There are many myths about quitting smoking. One of the most enduring, and misleading, is that it has to involve huge amounts of willpower. This is nonsense. Willpower is not is a good way to quit smoking or beat any other addiction. Let me explain why.

First of all, approaches based on willpower don't address the underlying cause of addiction. If you don't get to the root of the problem, you can't get to the root of the solution.

Secondly, 'willpower' means trying to make yourself do things you don't naturally *want* to do. After all, you never mention willpower when it comes to things you *want* to do, like watching your favourite show or tucking into a pizza. So, trying to give up smoking by willpower effectively means trying to make yourself do things that you don't want to do and that you *know* you don't want to do.

This leads to a very significant problem. The truth about willpower is that *it always runs out*. Nobody has an infinite supply. Your willpower might run out after a few days, weeks or months. It might run out after a year... but it *will* definitely run out.

I can even tell you *when* it's most likely to run out. The chances are, it will run out during your next emotional crunch point: a relationship goes wrong, you get frustrated at work, a friend lets you down and so on. If willpower is the tree, emotional crunch points are the chainsaw.

When your willpower runs out, as it certainly will, you will abandon the things you have been trying to make yourself do and go back to your old lifestyle — the lifestyle that led to you being a smoker and using tobacco to achieve certain changes in your emotional state of mind.

Fact: **willpower is no power**. It's not a way to *permanently* quit smoking because it's a *temporary* fix and always runs out. This is why none of the steps in Part One of this book rely on willpower or assume you have vast reserves of self-discipline.

The Mind/Computer Analogy

A common example of well-intentioned but misguided advice is the mind/computer analogy. If you're trying to overcome a bad habit — whether it's smoking or anything else — you're likely to meet people who say things like this:

> "You know, your mind is sort of like a computer. Think of the habit you're trying to change as a program that runs on the computer. What you have to do is reprogram your mind, or delete the old program and replace it with a new one."

This is wrong.

I have nothing against *helpful* analogies. However, the computer analogy is *not* useful if you're trying to stop smoking or overcome any other type of addiction. You can delete a computer program with the click of a mouse or a few keystrokes. It's so easy you can even do it by accident (as I have discovered, to my horror, several times in my life). Your brain simply doesn't work the same way. The 'hardware' is very different and we only have a very limited understanding of how it all works.

If you tell someone that getting rid of a bad habit should be as *easy* as deleting a computer file, and they repeatedly fail, this can create bad feelings. They may conclude they are inadequate — unable to do something you're saying *should* be as simple as clicking a mouse.

This is why I never use this type of analogy and try to avoid expressions such as 're-programming your mind'.

My Story

Personally, I blame Cupid.

Until I reached the ripe old age of 21, I had no interest in smoking whatsoever. None of my family smoked and even during my wild and rebellious teenage years (which were in fact pathetically tame) I had very few friends who smoked or thought it was 'cool'.

Everything changed in 1982, during my third year at university. One evening, at a social event, I met Harriet (all names have been changed to protect the culpable). She was smart, funny and beautiful, blessed with a dazzling mane of naturally auburn hair that hypnotised me from the word go. We talked our talk, she smiled her smile and I fell entirely under her spell. What's more, I later discovered she had a cassette tape of Mike Oldfield's 'Ommadawn' — the album that changed my life and means more to me than any other. It was clear that the universe meant for us to be together. (If younger readers want to go and look up what a 'cassette tape' was, it's okay, I'll wait.)

By any standards, Harriet was way out of my league. Every time I talked to her, which was as often as I could possibly contrive, it looked like Quasimodo serenading a swan. Nonetheless, I dared to believe I might win the romantic lottery. During my lectures, my meals, my sunrise and sighs, my time with friends and my dreams without end, I hoped that maybe one day pigs would fly, rain would fall upwards and Harriet would reciprocate my feelings.

On this occasion, the hoping worked rather well. Cupid twanged a few arrows and before long, in reckless defiance of all sense or reason, the breathtaking Harriet and I were an item. I didn't just have a girlfriend — my dear reader, I had *the* girlfriend.

Harriet's best friend, Anita, was a firecracker of energy and laughter who rapidly became my favourite bad influence. Her boyfriend, Gerard, was everything I wasn't: shrewd, cool, funny and macho in a stubbly James Dean sort of way. The four of us got along very well. Nothing mattered more to me than making sure I would 'fit in' with these three glorious new friends — all of whom smoked cigarettes.

Tempted though I was to try smoking, I decided to resist. I felt it was important to remain true to myself, knowing that my friends — if they were friends worth the name — would respect my decision. Calmly but assertively, I made it clear that while they could smoke if they wished to, and I wasn't judging them, I personally preferred *not* to smoke and hoped they would respect my choice. None of this is true.

I gave way like a tissue paper bridge in a monsoon. The first time Harriet tentatively enquired if I might, perhaps, like a cigarette, I accepted with ridiculous haste. My first smoke was a vile and disgusting experience, of course. However, being brave, fearless and foolish in the pursuit of true love, I soldiered on, manfully enduring one cigarette after another. Mock my frailty if you wish, but rhapsodically lush cascades of auburn hair do not come along every day.

We all have our personal addiction profile: highly susceptible to some addictions while largely immune to others. For example, I enjoy drinking now and again but alcohol can never control me. It's my occasional friend but never my master. With nicotine it was a slightly different story. It sank its fangs into me faster than a striking cobra. In fact, faster than the cobra that is known to his friends as 'Lightning Larry', has won the national 'Quick On The Fang' contest three years in a row, is an inspiration to countless young cobras and has his own range of merchandise, including T shirts, bumper stickers and, perhaps most bizarrely of all, cufflinks. Yes, it was *that* fast. With impressive agility, assisted by my tail-wagging desire to please the gorgeous Harriet, I made the leap from 'this is vile' to 'twenty a day' in a matter of weeks.

Not every student romance segues neatly into a lifetime of wedded bliss — not even ones fuelled by Mike Oldfield's majestic aural tapestries emanating from a cheap, hissy tape deck with fading batteries at two o'clock in the morning. After a gloriously happy year, my friends and I graduated and went our separate ways. Harriet, perhaps inevitably, found new love elsewhere. She left but the cigarettes stayed.

Finding a job was tricky, largely because I knew nothing and had no marketable skills (this is still the case). Via a series of outrageous flukes, I managed to eke out a living as a freelance writer. I worked here and there, moved around the country, did stuff, lived a little, loved a lot. Life was kind, times were good, days were bright. There were stumbles and bruises, as there always are, but the wounds healed quickly.

Tobacco was with me all the way: a resented crutch, treacherous servant, cackling killer. From time to time, I decided to quit. Always managed it, always went back. At my peak, I was on sixty cigarettes a day. How I survived, I'll never know.

There was always plenty of advice around about how to quit. The problem was that no-one ever told me how to neutralise the underlying addiction. You see, if you don't get to the root of the problem, you can't get to the root of the solution. I could temporarily *hide* from my addiction to nicotine, evade it, resist it... but it was always lurking within, waiting for a chance to re-surface (usually after an emotional crunch point of some kind) and once more make me its puppet.

My hunt for the answer led me to consult a lot of people, read a lot of books and try every method I'd ever heard of. Nothing worked because nobody told me how to reach into my mind and change the underlying mechanism of the addiction itself — the process I call the Want Fix.

I finally quit smoking for good in the year 2000. To say the least, this was a protracted and frustrating process. At the time, I didn't know about 'parts integration' and the 'Want Fix'. However, I had stumbled across some related ideas and started to focus on the difference between short-term fixes (that aren't really fixes at all since they never last) and a broader perspective that led to real, lasting solutions instead of comforting mirages and delusions. It was a slow process, but I was gradually able to change my *emotional* attitude towards smoking.

This still left me wondering how to overcome my physical dependency on nicotine. Fortunately, I came down with a particularly virulent bout of flu. It was the sort of flu that makes survival seem the *less* preferable option. For ten days, I couldn't do anything except feel wretched, ache all over and feel sorry for myself. I looked like a make-up test for 'The Exorcist'. During this thoroughly unpleasant time, I tried to smoke but found I was simply unable to do so. My wheezing, suppurating body just wouldn't take it. After three days of zero nicotine, I noticed that my dependency (like the rest of me) was broken.

When I eventually recovered from the flu, I simply never went back to smoking. Never wanted to, never will. In fact, I wouldn't want a cigarette now even if it were magically bereft of harmful consequences. That particular circuit just doesn't exist in my mind any more.

For years after I'd stopped smoking, the phenomenon of addiction continued to fascinate me (and I was, in any case, still dealing with a separate addiction, to sugar and starch, that had led to my being obese). How can so many of us, in so many different ways, be so prone to doing things that we know are unhealthy, harmful or even, in some cases, fatal? I wanted to understand all I could about this curious phenomenon. I started to put together the material that, in distilled form, became the basis for this book and my other books about addiction.

Some of this material came from my own experience plus a lot of reading and talking to people. Some of it came from other sources. For example, someone asked me to ghost-write their book about overcoming anxiety. This turned out to be a fascinating project from which I gained a few more valuable insights, particularly about what I now call the Want Fix. In addition, while teaching some of my public classes (about completely unrelated subjects) or speaking at conferences, I was lucky enough to meet various therapists who shared valuable advice. It took me more than a decade to put all this material together. This book is the result.

I don't know you or where you are on your journey through life, with all its sunshine and clouds, bright dawns and wistful sunsets, poetry and pain, golden hopes and jagged edges. What I do know is that you're on the amazing adventure called 'fulfilling your potential' and that you deserve the best this life has to offer.

I know you deserve more than to be the puppet of tobacco companies, hooked on a drug, ruining your health so they get rich while you get ill. They don't care about you. To them, you're just another set of lungs to be polluted, another mind to be stuffed with toxic propaganda.

What if it were time to start respecting and loving yourself? How about being *really* free, not just free to be a slave to a carcinogenic drug? How about giving yourself the best possible chance of staying healthy for as long as you can?

I don't know if I will ever sell more than a few copies of this book and I don't care. So long as it helps just *one* person to quit smoking, it will have been worth writing.

You're great. You're worth it. You can do it.

Final Words

We've reached the end of this book.

You now have all the information you need. You know about the Want Fix and the PAT Process. You know how to change how your Fixer works and makes you feel better. You also know how to break your dependency in just three days.

I hope you choose a new life and a new, non-smoking you. Live the healthiest and happiest life you can live, with vitality, energy and *lots* of people complimenting you on your success!

I believe in celebrating all that's best in this life. You deserve the best and you can have the best. The best relationship with your body, the fantastic feeling of health and the end of stress. You deserve all this and you can choose it for yourself.

If you want to get in touch, my email address is ian@ianrowland.com (or just visit any of my websites and use the email link provided). I'd love to hear from you.

— Ian Rowland

London, 2020

---

www.ianrowland.com
About my work as a writer-for-hire.

www.coldreadingsuccess.com
Everything to do with cold reading and 'cold reading for business'.

www.ianrowlandtraining.com
My talks and training for conferences, corporate groups and private clients.

End Note 1: An Invitation

Let's work together!

I offer talks and training for conferences, corporate groups and individuals, in real life or online. For details, please see: www.ianrowlandtraining.com.

I'd love to work with you.

— Ian Rowland

www.ianrowland.com
www.coldreadingsuccess.com
www.ianrowlandtraining.com

End Note 2: Three Requests

Please Help Me If You Can

If you'd like to support me and my work, please tell all your friends about this book and my various websites. I'm self-employed and promote my work as best I can, but a little help is always welcome. If you can help me to 'spread the word', I would be very grateful.

For example, you can mention me to your friends in real life or on social media. Wherever people are discussing addiction, weight loss or getting fit, please give me and my books a mention and pass on the link: www.ianrowlandtraining.com.

Got contacts in broadcast or online media? Tell them about me or about this book. They might get a good story, article or feature out of it — if you've got an audience, I've got content! Maybe you can help me to get media appearances or to get booked to give a talk or presentation. I'd appreciate whatever help you want to offer.

Improvements, Fixes And Flubs

If you have notes or ideas about how I can improve this book, or if you've noticed errors I should fix, I'd love to hear from you. If there are factual errors, things I should explain more clearly or typos, I'd love to correct them.

Please Send Me Your Review

Reviews are really helpful. If you can, please send me a review of this book that I can add to the product page on my website. My email address is ian@ianrowland.com . Your review can be published under your own name or can be as anonymous as you wish.

Your review doesn't have to very long or a literary masterpiece. Short reviews can be great although if you *want* to write a detailed review then you're welcome to do so! Also, don't worry if your writing needs a little help or tidying up. I can take care of that for you.

You can also submit reviews to Amazon if you obtained any of my books from there.

What Can I Do For You?

Personal Coaching And Training

I work with private clients all over the world, either in person or via the internet. Some people ask me for help with smoking or other addictions. Others want a little help with self-fulfilment and personal success, building their business, creating a passive income or related subjects. Let's work together and see what value I can provide for you!

See any of my websites for details.

Talks, Keynotes And Corporate Training

I love taking part in live events! I offer excellent talks, training and keynotes on subjects such as persuasion and communication skills, working for yourself, creating digital products and building a passive income. I often add touches of magic and mindreading, just to make my sessions a little bit different!

To date, I've worked for the FBI, Google, Coca-Cola, Marks & Spencer, The British Olympics Team, The Ministry of Defence, Hewlett-Packard, The Philadelphia 76ers, CapGemini, BBC, Kier Construction, NBC, The Crown Estate, Iceland, Medtronic, Unilever, The Sunday Times Oxford Literary Festival, The Prince's Charities, McKinsey & Company, Eurostar Software Testing Conference, Ogilvy & Mather, Rabobank, London Business School, ABC Television, Channel 4, Cambridge Technology Partners, Synon, Valtech and many other companies.

I've also lectured at Oxford University, Cambridge University, the California Institute of Technology and Monash University.

Writing

A friend once described me as 'a book midwife'. If you have a book in you, I'll help you to write it, publish it yourself, market it and make some money from it. I've been a professional writer for over 35 years and I offer a complete, end-to-end service.

I particularly like helping people to create a passive income for themselves: create a product, set up a website, make money while you sleep. This is what I've been doing for about twenty years. I can guide you through the entire process! It's a challenging road to travel, to be sure, but at the same time highly satisfying and rewarding.

Social Media

I'd love to stay in touch via social media!

For each of my main websites, there is a corresponding Facebook page:

www.ianrowland.com
www.coldreadingsuccess.com
www.ianrowlandtraining.com

You can also find me on:
Twitter (@IanRowland1)
Linked In
Instagram

Some Kind Words...

"My FBI Behavioural Analysis Program hired Ian to work with and train our team for a full day. He demonstrated and taught us a lot about cold reading and how we could apply it to our work as behavioural analysts. Additionally, he also covered advanced communication skills, persuasive language and relevant insights into the art of 'misdirection'. At the conclusion of his comprehensive seminar, he entertained our entire team and families with a mindreading show at an evening social. Not only was it great fun, but even today my team is still talking about it. I'd highly recommend Ian to anyone who's interested in these subjects and wants a first-class speaker and trainer."
— *Robin Dreeke, former Special Agent and Head of* **FBI Behavioural Analysis Program**

"I regard Ian as a first-rate trainer and consultant. He has amazing material, he always delivers and he's great to work with."
— *A. Sanghi, Lead Economist,* **World Bank Group**

"Ian has a very engaging and energising style and he was thought-provoking and entertaining throughout. Most importantly, everyone said it was a great use of their time. Ian gave us plenty of ways to work smarter and be more effective both professionally and personally."
— *A. Mellor,* **Marks & Spencer**

"Ian is the best speaker and trainer I've ever seen, and he hosted our day perfectly. We learned a lot, he was entertaining and I know we'll be more successful this year thanks to what he shared with us."
— *D. Holmes, Financial Director,* **Healthcare Learning**

"We had some of the top experts around the globe in their field, but when we looked at how people were registering for the conference and what the attendees wanted, overwhelmingly we saw very large numbers signing up for Ian's course, so much so that his class was the largest in the whole session that we had for those three days."
— *Chris Hadnagy,* **Organiser, Human Hacking Conference**

"Of the hundred plus lectures and shows we have hosted at Caltech none have brought more enthusiastic praise than your performance. I have now heard from dozens of people in the audience, all of whom said this was one of the most entertaining, informative, and above all funny shows they had ever seen. You are to be congratulated for breathing so much life and class into the science and skeptics community."
— *Michael Shermer,* **Executive Director, Skeptics Society**

"Ian's special talent lies in his ability to communicate useful information about self-improvement, business, psychology and, yes, magic to diverse audiences around the world. His books are essential reading and if you get the opportunity to hear him speak, don't miss him! For those outside the world of magic and mindreading, let me tell you that Ian is very highly regarded in the trade. He even gets hired to go to major conventions and teach other magicians! When I was Editor of the Magic Circle's magazine, I asked Ian to write a column on mindreading, which he did for 12 years to great acclaim."
— Matthew Field, **Member of the Inner Magic Circle**

"I've been an Independent Financial Advisor for 20 years and have learned from people like Dale Carnegie, Anthony Robbins, Jim Rohn and Brian Tracy. I now include Ian Rowland on that list. Having attended his courses and invested in some personal coaching with him, I cannot recommend him highly enough. His unique insights regarding positive persuasion and what makes people tick will prove invaluable in your personal and business life. He's funny, engaging and a leader in his field."
— Mike LeGassick, **Leading Independent Financial Advisor**, UK

"I make it my business to learn from experts. I spent four days with Ian and we covered a range of skills that I know will help me both personally and professionally — particularly inter-personal skills and ways to establish instant rapport with people. I think he's terrific."
— Sam Q., **Entrepreneur**, Saudi Arabia

"I'm a sales guy. I've studied all the big names and been trained by some of the best in the business. I trained with Ian via Skype and he just blew my mind with techniques and perspectives I never knew before. It's all practical. I use what Ian taught me almost every day. He opened my eyes to aspects of communication that truly deserve the term 'magic'."
— Michael Martin, **Sales professional**, USA

"I studied CRFB with Ian via Skype and without doubt it's my best investment this year! Ian is an excellent teacher and working with him is very enjoyable. In addition, Ian is incredibly generous with his knowledge in many adjacent fields.
— Patrick Ehrich, **Teacher and Educational Trainer**, Germany

Love And Gratitude

I want to place on record my thanks to everyone who has contributed to this book in one way or another.

Liam O'Neill, also known as 'The Prove-It Guy', has been and continues to be a terrific source of inspiration, advice and fun. If you want to know anything about health, diet, fitness and exercise, he's *the* man to see.

Julia Cotterill provided invaluable help during the development of my 'Addiction Fixer' website and all the books associated with it. Her very thorough notes and constructive criticism proved tremendously useful.

James Mallinson explained 'Parts Integration' to me, from his perspective as a knowledgeable and highly experienced hypnotherapist, and provided helpful guidance.

AJ Green, who has been a good friend for many years and has worked with me on numerous projects, was very supportive during the development of the 'Addiction Fixer' website.

Federica Finello provided the Italian translation in the section on Time Re-allocation.

Laylah Garner assisted me with the cover design. She's an excellent graphic designer who has often helped me over the years. Simon Craze helped me with the 'wordtoons' that appear in this book.

Barry Cooper did the proofreading and did it very well. He gets the credit for everything that's right while I take the blame for anything that's wrong.

www.ingramcontent.com/pod-product-compliance
Lightning Source LLC
Chambersburg PA
CBHW071202090426
42736CB00012B/2425